What Is God?

also by John F. Haught
published by Paulist Press

THE COSMIC ADVENTURE

What Is God?

How To Think About the Divine

John F. Haught

PAULIST PRESS
New York/Mahwah

Library of Congress
Catalog Card Number: 85-62872

ISBN: 0–8091–2754–7

Published by Paulist Press
997 Macarthur Boulevard
Mahwah, New Jersey 07430

Printed and bound in the
United States of America

Contents

*To my Colleagues in the
Theology Department at Georgetown*

Introduction

Let us not ask immediately "who" God is, but instead "what" God is. "What is God?" may seem, however, to be a peculiar question. For most theists, at least, it seems more natural to ask "who" God is. Certainly this is how biblical religion puts the question, for example, when Moses asks, "Who shall I say has sent me?" The sense of God as a personal subject has held primacy in Western religious experience.

The perspective of critical inquiry, however, must ask "what?" Thinkers ask questions like "What is nature?" "What is man?" "What is time?" "What is space?" "What is history?" "What is the universe?" etc. They cannot help asking also, "What is God?"

The topic of this book is how to *think* about God. God is not an easy subject to think about, let alone write about. If we are interested in referring to God at all it is probably because we have had a "feeling," a "premonition," a "sense" or "intuition" of what is referred to as God. But feelings, premonitions and sensations are not yet what I mean by thought. Even though the term may have a much broader application, by thought I mean here the *theoretical*

What Is God?

mode of consciousness. By theoretical consciousness I mean the type of cognition in which we step back from the immediacy of an experience and place that experience in a conceptual framework. Once we have placed our immediate experience in such a network of ideas the original experience can be mediated to us in a way that allows us to relate it to other experiences and ideas.

There are religious "thinkers" who insist that God can only be addressed as a subject and cannot be made the object of human thought. Any possible encounter with the divine, they say, can occur only in worship and prayer but not in theoretical attempts to describe what God may be like. And there are strong elements in both Eastern and Western religious traditions that support this "negative theology." They teach us that we may say what God is *not* but not what God is.

On the other hand equally persuasive aspects of theological traditions insist that some sort of positive reference to the divine is possible, though of course our language is always inadequate at best. This "positive theology" allows us at least to use analogies in our discourse about that which is unthinkable. Religious symbolism, used by all the traditions, is already analogous language, and this symbolism inevitably arouses in us the need to think and theorize about that to which it points. Hence, provided that we constantly keep in mind the deficiencies of our metaphors and ideas of the ultimate, we are allowed and even required to *think* about the divine.

The idea of God is not an invention of theory but the product of a unique type of experience. Philosophers did not invent the notion of God. It came to human consciousness and insinuated itself into history by way of the spontaneous life of religious people. The original language in which it appeared is that of symbol and myth. And it was acted out in ritual and other kinds of human activity long before it became a topic of philosophical or theological discussion. Hence any reflection that we undertake in our theoretical mode must refer again and again to these "naive" expressions. For it may be that in these symbolic sources there is an ever renewable plenitude of meaning that can continue to nourish our thinking in every age, no matter how scientifically minded we may become.[1]

Yet even this is not enough for any attempt to think about God. For any meaningful theoretical reflection on the idea of God must also take into account our own experience as well. We must ask whether there is anything identifiable in the experience of *all* of us, and not just "religious" people, to which the name "God" might possibly refer. Unless there is some common ground of reference when people speak of the divine, then such discourse may be humanly meaningless. If people do not already, in their ordinary life experience, have at least a vague sense of the region of reality to which the name "God" is possibly alluding, then it seems pointless to speak to them of the divine at all. In order for our language to make any sense it must light up some area that has already been at least dimly intuited by those we are addressing. Otherwise our words bear no meaning whatsoever. But is there any such common region of human experience that might possibly be illuminated by our speaking of "God"?

It has become a matter of dispute whether the word "God" refers to any realistic aspect of our experience at all. Skeptical thinkers suggest that we should resign ourselves at this time in our history to the conjecture that all talk about God is obsolete, a leftover from the childhood of the human race, a mere projection of wishful thinking, the product of oppressive socio-economic conditions, or a stopgap for human ignorance and weakness. This book is writ-

ten for all those who may have been tempted to adopt one
or other aspect of this suspicion. This readership includes
not only skeptics, but also people who consider themselves
believers. For even the latter, if they are honest, have to
admit that the above possibilities have at least occasionally
crossed their own minds as well.

In this book I shall suggest five ways of thinking realistically about God. I shall propose that "God" need not be
mistaken as referring to anything alien to the deepest
aspects of our common human experience. And I shall
argue that the referent of this name is what *all* of us have
already experienced to one degree or another, and what we
all long to experience even more intimately at the most fundamental levels of our being. If each of us were capable of
excavating the deepest layers of our desire, "God" would
make sense as an appropriate name for the objective of this
desire. And if this seems too easy, since the mere desire for
something in no way constitutes evidence of its reality, I
shall go further. In Chapter 5 I shall propose that if we honestly come into touch with the very *deepest* level of our
desiring, then the idea of God may be affirmed not only as
satisfying but as truthful as well.

Today, however, there is a serious question among scientific thinkers, philosophers and many other intelligent
people as to whether the word "God" actually refers to any
genuinely real dimension of our experience. The suspicion
that one finds in the writings of Nietzsche, Marx and Freud
is shared by many intellectuals today. And it has occurred
to numerous thoughtful and sincere people that talk about
"God" is at best little more than a heartwarming whistling
in the dark, and at worst a cover-up for human weakness
or ideological selfishness. Given the way in which the idea
of God has been employed by many "religious" people,
such suspicion is often justified. But the word "God" can

mean much more than this, and I shall attempt to show several ways in which, without sacrificing our critical faculties, we may find a referent for this name within the horizon of our own experience.

I shall attempt this location of transcendence by asking you to reflect on five ordinary aspects of your own life experience: your experience of depth, future, freedom, beauty and truth. We have all experienced these to one degree or another, but in some way they also lie beyond our grasp. While there is something undeniably "real" about all of these aspects of conscious existence, there is something very elusive about them as well. On the one hand we long for these eminent realities, but on the other hand we find them too much for us, and so we turn our faces away from their blinding light. If we reflect on the ambivalent attitude that we have toward these dimensions of experience, we may find a pattern identical to the one scholars have found in their studies of how religious people respond to the sense of the "sacred." Though the sacred is not an explicit ingredient in the experience of some people today—it certainly still seems to be explicit in that of the majority of non-intellectuals—there is nevertheless something within the scope of their awareness that still presents itself in the same way as what Rudolf Otto called the *mysterium tremendum et fascinans*.[2] There is much that is questionable in Otto's famous analysis of religious experience, but I think that his characterization of the ambivalent responses we have to the ineffable margins of our existence is fundamentally correct. We react to depth, future, freedom, beauty and truth in the same way that Otto's *homo religiosus* reacts to the "sacred." We experience these realities first of all as *mysteria*, that is, as incomprehensible, overwhelming, majestic. They evoke in us a sense of reverence and awe. Secondly, they are *tremenda* in that they are terrifying in their demands upon us, and so understandably we shrink from them, fearing that we shall be lost if we surrender completely to them. But finally they are *fascinosa*, inasmuch as there is something ultimately fascinating, seductive, attractive and satisfying about them. They have the same features Otto saw in the religious experience of the sacred. I think his analysis is still appropriate to an understanding of the five elements we shall be focusing on in the chapters that follow.

When people hear the word "God," however, they usually associate it with a human-like image of a cosmic "personality." One of the most difficult problems in philosophical and theological discussion is whether it is appropriate to think of God as personal, and, if so, according to which specific gender. Many people have trouble intellectually with the apparently anthropomorphic, and, in a scientific age, with the seeming irrationality of belief in a personal God. We may recall, in this connection, Albert Einstein's rejection of the idea of a personal God as primitive superstition. Though the famous physicist considered himself to be "religious," in the sense of adopting an attitude of reverential submission to the mysteriousness of the universe, he could not reconcile the "personality" of God with his conception of modern science. On the other hand, most worshipers find it difficult to relate to a cosmic principle that appears totally impersonal.

I am unable to deal here with the complexities of this problem. But I shall proceed under the assumption that a transcendent reality that does not possess at the very least those qualities which constitute the dignity of human persons, that is, something like intelligence, feeling, freedom, power, initiative, creativity, etc. (though to an eminent degree), could not adequately inspire trust or reverence in human beings. In this sense God would have to be "personal" to be God. It is doubtful whether believers could be fully satisfied religiously by surrendering to something that is less intense in being than they are, that is, to something that does not have at least the stature of personality (which is the most intense form of being of which we have any direct experience).

At the same time, however, personality does not fully express what we mean by God either. There is also a transpersonal or superpersonal aspect to God according to significant strands of many religious traditions. Religions often allude to an aspect of deity that cannot be adequately represented in personalistic imagery. And it is this side of "thought" about God that I shall highlight. I must emphasize this aspect in order to make sense of the main problem associated with talk about God, namely, God's apparent absence and unavailability.

Throughout the following chapters I shall try to keep one eye on the gnawing question that both non-believers and believers in God have always had about the divine absence: if God is a reality, why is this reality so unavailable, so unverifiable, so elusive? Why, as Freud asked, should that which holds the most importance for believers, namely God, be so lacking in immediate obviousness to themselves as well as to non-believers? I shall contend that an examination of the transpersonal dimension of God's life, that side of God's being which cannot be fully represented in personalistic terms, may help us to make some sense of the "scandal" of the divine hiddenness.

Hence I shall be referring less to "God" than to "the divine." I shall be accentuating the "neuter" more than the masculine and feminine images evoked by religious symbolism. It seems important that we counterbalance such anthropomorphic imagery with a neuter language if our topic is the "whatness" of God. Hans-Georg Gadamer relates how his teacher, the great philosopher Martin Heidegger, once observed: "Who is God? That is perhaps beyond the possibilities of our asking. But what is God? That we should ask." And Gadamer thinks that attention to the neuter expression "the divine" may give breadth to our ideas of transcendence:

> Notice the neuter: "the divine." I think the neuter is one of the most mysterious things in human language wherever it is preserved. German and Greek have the excellence of preserving the neuter. The neuter occurs very often in poetry. What is the neuter? To use the neuter—for example, "the beautiful"; in German *das Schoene*; in Greek *to kalon*—expresses something of ungraspable presence. It is no longer "this" or "that," male or female, here or there; it is like filling empty space. . . . The neuter represents in a way the plenitude of presence, the omnipresence of something. Hence the divine is indeed an expression for such omnipresence.[3]

Accordingly I shall represent "the divine" by way of generic aspects of our experience such as depth, future, freedom, beauty and truth. Thinking of the ultimate context of our existence in such a neuter manner seems necessary if we are to avoid unduly narrow ideas of ultimacy. There is a strong temptation in all historical religions to reduce their notions of God to manageable anthropomorphic proportions for the sake of easy access to and even control of deity. Thus an emphasis on the neuter in our thinking of God, while inadequate in itself, is a necessary corrective to a one-sidedly personalistic understanding.

Another more immediate reason for our dwelling on the neuter arises from the contemporary discussions among theists concerning the masculinity or femininity of God. At times these discussions have become heated to the point of hostility, and one wonders whether important aspects of the divine are not perhaps left out of the alternatives that are offered. While the controversy is an important one, it may distract us momentarily from the fact that significant aspects of our thinking about God do not require our opting for one or other of the two sexes as our primary model for symbolizing deity. Transcending the entire issue of gender is the encompassing horizon of "mystery" to which the following chapters attempt to provide a simple introduction. It is important today especially, now that the issue of God's sexuality has become so prominent in theological discussion, that we not forget that our quest for depth, future, freedom, beauty and truth is more fundamental than the specifically theistic concern as to whether God should be understood as male or female.

Finally, I shall keep my other eye on the question of how, in the light of our five ways of looking at the idea of God, we might understand the equally puzzling phenomenon called "religion." Each of the five following chapters will have three tasks: first, a theoretical discussion of the idea of God in terms of a specific dimension of our human experience; second, an understanding of why God does not show up as one object among others within this field of experience, that is, why God is by definition unavailable to any verificational control; third, how we might reach a deeper understanding of "religion" in the light of our analysis of these aspects of our experience.

As regards the latter, I shall discuss religion in a normative rather than descriptive manner. That is, I shall present an idealized picture of religion as it would exist if our response to the ultimate corresponded to the idea of God presented in each chapter. In actuality religion always falls short of realizing its essential nature, but since my method is not that of history or the social sciences, it is not necessary that I dwell on the obvious deviations or perversions that can be found in concrete "religious" life. Further, my discussion of religion will be limited by the obviously theistic point of departure I have taken. Nevertheless, in attempting to give breadth to the idea of God by thinking in neuter terms of "the divine," I hope that my reflections will also be able at least partially to interpret non-theistic religious experience as well.

The following chapters are a reworking of the reflections of some important religious thinkers of this century who have made significant contributions to our understanding of "the divine." Such notable authors as Paul Tillich, Alfred North Whitehead, Paul Ricoeur, Bernard Lonergan, Karl Rahner and numerous others have influenced the ideas presented here. I am deeply indebted to them all.

Chapter 1
Depth

In relating to another person, whoever it might be, but especially if it is someone I love, I may observe the following: sooner or later the other person will do something or say something that will surprise me. It may either delight or disappoint me. But if I am to sustain my relationship with the "other" I will have to revise my impressions of him or her. I will have to move to a deeper level of understanding the other. And after relating to the other person on this level for a while I will find occasion after occasion to dig still deeper. Of course I may resist the invitation to look deeper, and perhaps for the most part I do resist it. But it takes very little experience of other persons to see that there is something beneath the surface of my impressions of them. Other people are not what they seem to be. This is, of course, a truism so obvious that it seems almost too trivial even to mention. But perhaps there is more to it than first appears. Let us dig deeper.

Not only are others not what they seem to be, but the same is true of myself. There is always more to me than is contained in my impressions of myself. My "self-image" does not exhaust what I am. I need not be an expert in depth psychology in order to validate this observation. I need only a little experience of living to be able to see its truth. Looking back a few years, or even a few months or days, I remember that I thought I knew who I was. But new experiences have reshaped my life. New questions, new feelings and moods, new dreams and fantasies, new expectations of myself have intervened. I now know that I am not what I thought I was. I may assume at this moment that I am not exactly what I seem to be to myself or to others. Why is this so? Why are others not what they seem to be? Why am I not transparent to myself? This is a troubling question, so disturbing in fact that I usually suppress it. I cling to impressions as though they were foundational truths. I resist going deeper. Why?

Let us also take note of the fact that the natural and social worlds present superficial impressions of themselves that we must question. They too are not what they seem to be. In the case of nature the point is easily made by looking at science. Not only religion but also science thrives on the conviction that things are not what they seem to be. For example, beneath the world of common sense impressions there is a submicroscopic universe of "counterintuitive" physical occurrences that we cannot picture or even imagine. And in the galaxies beyond us there are likewise unfathomable riches of physical phenomena that, if we could understand them, would expose our world of immediate appearances and impressions as a veil of superficiality. We recoil from the abyss that lies beneath the surface of present knowledge, however, and live under the illusion that our sense impressions or our ordinary experiences of space and time are absolutely valid. And even scientists tend to cling tenaciously to their pet paradigms and models in an effort to domesticate science's tempestuous inner voice: "Things are not what they seem to be"—even after we have gone deeper and yet deeper in our understanding. The question keeps forcing itself upon us, therefore: Why are things not what they seem to be? What *is* reality that in the case of others, myself and nature it continually evades full disclosure? Why is it that what seemed profound yesterday is today exposed as trivial, or that what impressed me as deep before appears now as rather shallow? What sort of universe are we dealing with if it does not exhaust itself in our impressions of it?

And there is also the social world of institutions, politics, economic arrangements and their history. In this world that we share in common with others we may once again experience the shallowness of our impressions of things. Though peoples and nations can survive for years and even centuries on the assumption that their own social and cultural ideals and experiences are universally normative, sooner or later the events of history will bring about a serious challenge to this prejudice. The resistance to revisions of perspective will prove to be enormous, and people will even go to war to defend the alleged finality of their culture, politics or economics. But eventually they will have to confess: "We are not what we thought we were. Our previous self-understanding has been superficial and misguided. We must rethink what we are as a society." And so from a new perspective, occasionally at least, they may look back with amazement at their previous lack of sensitivity regarding their social and political life.

Let us return to our question, then: Why is it that in the case of others, myself, nature and society, things never are quite what they seem to be? According to Paul Tillich it is because there lies beneath their surface an infinite and inexhaustible *dimension of depth*[1] Perhaps many people would be content to call it a dimension of mystery. But this word, like the word "God" itself, has lost its meaning for many people. And so it might be useful in this context to call this dimension of inexhaustibility beneath the surface of our impressions simply the depth of existence, the depth of reality, the depth of the universe.

In his famous meditation, "The Depth of Existence," Tillich notes that the wisdom of all ages and continents tells us about the road to that depth. What gives the great classics of philosophy, literature and religion their authority generation after generation is that they are the expression of a journey toward depth undertaken by sincere and concerned individuals or peoples throughout history. The reason that they still grip us today is that we sense in them the call of a depth dimension that promises to give more substance to our lives than what we can find on the surface. They hold out the possibility to us that our own lives can be enriched and that an unexpected contentment with life can be ours if we follow them through the difficult but rewarding way to depth. Those whose lives and experiences have been imprinted in the great classics have all witnessed the same experience:

> They have found that they were not what they believed themselves to be, even after a deeper level had appeared to them below the vanishing surface. That deeper level itself became surface, when a still deeper level was discovered, this happening again and again, as long as their very lives, as long as they kept on the road to their depth.[2]

What name, then, can we give to this dimension of depth?

> The name of this infinite and inexhaustible depth . . . is *God*. That depth is what the word *God* means. And if

that word has not much meaning for you, translate it,
and speak of the depths of your life. . . . Perhaps, in
order to do so, you must forget everything traditional
that you have learned about God, perhaps even that
word itself. For if you know that God means depth you
know much about Him. You cannot then call yourself
an atheist or unbeliever. For you cannot think or say:
Life has no depth! Life itself is shallow. Being itself is
surface only. If you could say this in complete seriousness, you would be an atheist; but otherwise you are
not. He who knows about depth knows about God.[3]

This dimension of depth, therefore, will be the first of
five ideas in terms of which I would suggest that we think
about the divine.

What is there in the experience of all of us to which the
word "God" is pointing? Tillich's answer is that "God" is a
name for the dimension of depth that all of us experience
to one degree or another, even if only in the mode of flight
from it. We truly experience the depth even though we find
it impossible to focus on it as if it were just one other object
of vision or of scientific investigation. Depth appears more
as the *horizon* of our experience than as a direct object
thereof. Its apparent elusiveness is quite compatible with its
being the very condition of all of our experience. Perhaps,
as we shall see in more detail a bit later, this observation
can help us interpret, and tolerate, the apparent absence of
God. As the geographical horizon is unavailable to us since
it recedes as we explore further, so God might be understood in part as the ultimate horizon of all of our experience, always receding, encompassing, illuminating, but
never falling within our comprehending grasp. But in thinking of the divine as the ultimate "horizon" rather than as a
controllable object of experience, have we diminished our
sense of its reality?

There is a fundamental dimension of human experience that has the peculiar characteristic of being too massive and, let us say it, *too real*, to be trivialized as a specific object capable of being placed under our comprehending gaze. It is more accurate to say that this dimension comprehends us than that we comprehend it. We experience this dimension as real even though it is unavailable to our verificational control. In our frustration at not being able to comprehend it we may be tempted to deny that it exists at all, but this is a futile denial. All we have to do is to recall those moments in our personal life, in our relations with others, nature and society when we have been rocked from the surface by something that we could not control. We may have called it "fate" or "circumstance," and we may have cursed it or repressed it. But it would be hard to deny that there was something eminently real about the experience. It is as though something much larger than ourselves and our lives, or even our period of history, swept us into its embrace, even though we may have been tempted to think of such events as utterly impersonal and as in no way evidence of any sort of providentially divine care governing the course of our lives or of history. Taken in isolation these experiences may have constituted for us sufficient evidence of the universe's fundamental indifference to us.

However, there may also have been some moments after experiencing these "earthquakes" when we found ourselves on more solid ground than previously. The experience of "fate" was also one that led to a deeper "grounding" in reality. We may even have reached the point of being grateful that we went through difficult straits since they turned out to be the occasion of growth and a contentment that transcends mere gratification.[4] They have made us experience a new level of ourselves and reality. Such earthquakes awakened in us a courage that gave us a deeper sense of being alive. The dimension of depth, there-fore, is ambiguous. It is both terrifying and deeply fulfilling. In the words of Rudolf Otto, it is a *mysterium tremendum et fascinans.*

The experience of depth has two faces.[5] It is both abyss and ground. The dimension of depth which supports the surface of our lives initially presents itself to us as an *abyss.* Instinctively we recoil from an abyss since it seems to be unfathomable, bottomless, a void in which there are seem-ingly no supports. To fall into it would mean to lose our-selves. This is the first face the depth presents to us. It is an anxiety-inducing "nothingness" which seems to threaten our very being.

We might gain a more concrete sense of what this abyss means if we conjure up the specter of being utterly alone without the support of other people or of status or possessions. There is probably nothing we humans find more terrifying or try more ardently to avoid than the state of aloneness. One of the reasons for our anxiety about death is that it is an occurrence that we shall have to go through utterly alone. And so we tend to avoid the threat of death, along with other such "existential" threats as meaninglessness and guilt, since it signifies an intolerable solitariness. We bury our lives in objects, persons and pur-suits that seem to offer us a refuge from the abyss of aloneness.

What would happen, though, if we allowed ourselves, or were forced by "circumstances," to plunge into the abyss? Again the wisdom of those seekers of depth whose insights are buried in the classic texts of our great traditions has some encouragement for us that is worth pondering. They tell us over and over, whether in myth or direct phil-osophical and theological language, that there is yet another side to the depth. The depth will show itself to us

not only as an abyss, but also as *ground*. In the final analysis, the depth is ultimate support, absolute security, unrestricted love, eternal care. Compared to this ultimate
grounding of our existence, we are told, our ordinary supports are shallow, or at least inadequate. Hence there is
nothing to fear after all in loosening our grip on these supports and allowing ourselves to be swept into the depths of
our life. The reason we can have the courage to open ourselves to the depth, to accept our solitude, is that there is an
ultimate ground to our existence, there is an ultimate com-
panionship in our aloneness. The abyss is only one side of
the experience of depth, and we are tempted to think, as are
some important philosophers (like Nietzsche, Sartre and
Camus) that this is the only side. Most philosophers, and
all the major religious traditions, however, have insisted
that the final word about the depth is "trustworthy."[6] It is,
in Tillich's words, the "ground of our being."

A vivid expression of this sense of an ultimate salvific
ground within the lonely abyss of depth is given by Oscar
Wilde in an autobiographical account of his imprisonment:

> I bore up against everything with some stubbornness of
> will and much rebellion of nature, till I had absolutely
> nothing left in the world but one thing. I had lost my
> name, my position, my happiness, my freedom, my
> wealth. I was a prisoner and a pauper. But I still had
> my children left. Suddenly they were taken away from
> me by the law. It was a blow so appalling that I did not
> know what to do, so I flung myself on my knees, and
> bowed my head, and wept, and said, "The body of a
> child is as the body of the Lord: I am not worthy of
> either." That moment seemed to save me. I saw then
> that the only thing for me was to accept everything.
> Since then—curious as it will no doubt sound—I have

been happier. It was of course my soul in its ultimate essence that I had reached. In many ways I have been its enemy, but I found it waiting for me as a friend.[7]

This citation is from Wilde's *De Profundis*, "Out of the Depths." It has a decidedly "religious" quality to it, but testimony to the same experience of a ground on the other side of the abyss may be found also in the writings even of those thinkers who have absolutized the void and rejected the reality of any ultimate meaning. For example, Nietzsche, on the occasion of his horrifying vision of the eternal recurrence (according to which all moments of experience are destined to recur an infinite number of times), spoke of something in himself that he called "courage" which he said allowed him to accept his vision of this abyss.[8] This experience implies that there is more to depth than just abyss. There is also the courage to accept the abyss. Though he does not discuss where this courage comes from, Nietzsche's sense of its presence is an intimation of something like a ground in the depths of the abyss. This sensitive man felt beneath his culture and his own life a horrifying void, but he also found it impossible to suppress the hope for a new beginning. Such hope is inseparable from an at least inarticulate sense of grounding.

It is this ground of courage, testified to even by serious atheistic thinkers, that helps us in part to indicate what we mean by God. The reader may have experienced occasions in his or her own life when, facing a seemingly impossible challenge, an unanticipated influx of strength made it possible to go on. In such experiences one may have felt a surge of vitality that is absent in less urgent moments. What "God" means may, in part at least, be hinted at when we ask for the ultimate whence of this courage and vitality.[9]

The Absence of God

One of the most persistent aspects of the "problem of God" is that there is no unambiguous evidence in our ordinary experience of any providential, transcendent divine presence. Many so-called atheists point to this fact and wonder how any truly intelligent person can be a believer. Our point here, though, has been that the reality of God is no less capable of immediate validation than is the dimension of depth that underlies all of the impressions the world makes upon us. Therefore, that God is not easily accessible to our senses or to our whims and wishes should be no more of a scandal than that the dimension of depth is incapable of being brought under our comprehending control. That God cannot be brought into objectifying focus is no more remarkable than that the source of our courage is not always as available to us as are tools and other manipulable objects of our experience. God is not one object among others in our experience. Rather, God may be understood as the ultimate horizon which makes all of our experience possible in the first place. Therefore, it may not be appropriate for us to speak of an "experience" of God, if we mean "experience" in the ordinary sense of the term. God's presence is unobtrusive. The divine does not force itself into the range of objects or events that make up the content of our ordinary experience. Instead, God may be "thought of" as the inexhaustible depth and ground out of which all of our experiences arise. We continually dwell in this depth without focusing upon it. Because it evades our focal knowledge we may not often, or even ever, advert to its overwhelming presence.[10] But it is consistent with its humility and self-withdrawal that it does not force itself into the realm of vivid objects of our experience. It is the enabling condition, rather than the focal object, of our experience. The realm of objects that we are able to objectify or focus on is too narrow to contain the reality of the transcendent horizon of our experience. Thus the absence and unavailability of the divine from the realm of tangible and verifiable objects of knowledge provides no warrant for denying the reality of God.

Religion

The wisdom of the great traditions teaches us that the experience of depth often occurs after or within the experience of despair, disgrace, impoverishment, loss, suffering and especially the threat of death. Tillich summarizes this wisdom when he says," . . . there can be no depth without the way to depth. Truth without the way to truth is dead. . . ."[11] This "way" involves the experience of pain and loss, but also joy and ecstasy. It is only because we sense somehow that in the depth lies joy that we have the incentive to abandon ourselves to the abyss. We surmise that beneath the surface there is something that does not disappoint and that can bring a kind of contentment that runs deeper and endures longer that the usual forms of consolation we seek. This sense gives rise to religion. Religion is the passionate search for depth and for an ultimately solid ground to support our existence.

In the simplest terms, then, religion may be understood as the search for depth. To those who think that religion's only function is to provide answers this may seem to be an unusual and even unacceptable way of understanding religion. However, once we acknowledge that the dimension of depth is inexhaustible we must also confess that no present state of understanding can ever adequately represent this dimension. There is always a "more" that goes infinitely beyond what we have already grasped. Our relationship to this transcendent depth can never be one of mastery or possession. Indeed, to attempt such an absorption of the infinite horizon of our existence into the scope of our knowledge is repudiated by all the explicitly religious traditions as a deviation from authentic life. Instead the appropriate attitude to take with respect to the depth is that of waiting and searching.

But religion is more than a search. For religion is also a confident *naming* of the dimension of depth. It is the jubilant enunciation of a sense that the depth has broken through into our lives in one way or another. Religion is the symbolic (and at times ritualistic) expression of the shared experience of this depth that has made itself transparent to human consciousness. In order for us to undertake the adventurous quest which we have called religion we already need at least some sense of what we are seeking. Otherwise we would not be aroused to seek it at all. Somehow or other the depth has already insinuated itself into our lives at the same time that it has elusively receded into the distance. One way in which it makes itself provisionally known to us is to embody itself in events, persons or aspects of nature and history. These then function as *symbols* that inspire us to trust and that motivate us to look deeper. Religion, therefore, is a surrender to those symbols and stories that give us the courage to seek further.

It is a tragic error of religious education to give people the impression that the conversion to a specific set of symbols or doctrines is the end of life's adventure into the unknown. Instead, "conversion" can mean a new turn and a new confidence in the unending journey to the depth of our lives. It is a commitment to undertake the quest with an irreversible trust. Such conversion may give us a "certitude" that makes us want to share our confidence with others, and so religion takes on a communal, social (and inevitably institutional) aspect, the purpose of which is to facilitate and not to impede the process of sharing the experience of reality's depth. But the certitude we share with others must never be misconstrued (though it often is, nonetheless) as a possession. Once again Tillich has some profound words of caution for those who try to turn God, understood as the depth of existence, into a possession:

> The condition of man's relation to God is first of all one of *not* having, *not* seeking, *not* knowing, and *not* grasping. A religion in which that is forgotten, no matter how ecstatic or active or reasonable, replaces God by its own creation of an image of God. . . . It is not easy to endure this not having God, this waiting for God. . . . For how can God be possessed? Is God a thing that can be grasped and known among other things? Is God less than a human person? We always have to wait for a human being. Even in the most intimate communio.. among human beings, there is an element of *not* having and *not* knowing, and of waiting. Therefore, since God is infinitely hidden, free, and incalculable, we must wait for Him in the most absolute and radical way. He is God for us just in so far as we do *not* possess Him. . . . We have God through *not* having Him.[12]

This view of religious existence recognizes that "there can be no depth without the way to depth."[13] The fulfillment of our deepest longings cannot occur in one instantaneous act of consciousness, though perhaps a radical decision to live irreversibly in trustful waiting may be one that takes place in single moment. The experience of God as depth involves our embarking on a way, a journey, a pilgrimage with the full awareness that the end of it may lie an infinite distance ahead. Radical waiting is, of all possible responses to our life, the most difficult, the most arduous, the most ungratifying. But it is also, as Tillich says, the most realistic and the most fulfilling, the one that takes the depth most seriously. And it is not as though by this waiting and searching we are deprived of strength to endure joyfully in the present:

> If we wait in hope and patience, the power of that for which we wait is already effective within us. He who waits in absolute seriousness is already grasped by that for which he waits. He who waits in patience has already received the power of that for which he waits. He who waits passionately is already an active power himself, the greatest power of transformation in personal and historical life. We are stronger when we wait than when we possess.[14]

In summary, if God is the depth of existence, then religion is the confident search for this depth as well as the celebration of those events, persons or occasions where the depth has broken through the surface of our lives in an exceptional way. The test of whether we are religious or not is simply whether we are concerned with this dimension of depth. And it is the degree of seriousness whereby we ask ultimate questions, and not the degree of doctrinal certitude, that determines whether we are surrendering to the transcendent depth of our lives, that is, to God.

Chapter 2
Future

Again let us start with the obvious. I would invite the reader to pause now and attend to the transient character of this moment. Notice how impossible it is to hold on to it, how it slips out of your grasp. Where did it go? It was present a few moments ago, but now its presentness has been lost and another present has slipped into its place. When the earlier moment vanished, did it slip into nothingness? Did it undergo an absolute perishing? The very fact that you can recall it, that it still persists in your memory is evidence that it did not perish utterly. In some fashion or other it still lives on. What we call the "past" is the repository of all those formerly present moments whose immediacy has now been lost to us and which have the enduring status of "having been."

For now, though, our focus is not the past. We know that the formerly present moment took up a permanent dwelling in the past. But where did it come from in the first place? That edge of freshness that blended into a present experience lived only for a moment and then perished. Where did it come from? The source of that moment's novelty we refer to as the *future*.

It is impossible for us to define the future. We cannot hold it out before us as an object of tangible grasp. It evades our comprehension. But we cannot avoid experiencing it or being affected by it. We cannot deny that the future, any more than the dimension of depth, is a part of our experience, even though we cannot bring it into focus. We are constantly being "invaded" by it, "overwhelmed" by it, "carried into" it, or we are simply trying to avoid it. The future is clearly an ineluctable aspect of our experience and not an illusion, though it is too elusive to be turned into an object for our examination in the same sense as, for example, a physical object in front of our eyes. There is something very slippery about the future. But even though it cannot be reified, there is still something inevitable about it.

If there is anything in our ordinary experience that lies beyond our control it is the relentless conquering of the present by the future. Again, this is so obvious as not to need mentioning. But our approach in each chapter of this book is to begin with the obvious. We start with those experiences which are so matter-of-fact, so taken for granted, that we find it difficult even to talk about them. Certainly futurity is one of the commonplaces that evades our ordinary focal understanding. It is a dimension that our consciousness dwells in without usually focusing on. Indeed, focusing on it as we are doing now is likely to distort the understanding and feeling of it that we have in our spontaneous existence. Nonetheless, we must ask an unusual, strange-sounding question about it: What is the future? Perhaps the reader has never been confronted by such an apparently inane question before. After all, this kind of question seems to fall into the same context as other apparently unanswerable puzzles such as: What is matter? What is reality? What is nature? What is truth? What is beauty?

Similarly the question "What is the future?" generates at first glance little apparent hope for a clear or interesting answer.

Yet we may wisely follow Tillich's suggestion that the greatest breakthroughs in human consciousness take place when we learn to question what we had previously taken for granted and had not asked about before. And such inquiry usually occurs only when there has been some sort of breakdown, some failure of that which we had previously taken for granted. A sudden interest in things we have taken for granted is aroused as soon as they vanish or are threatened. As we saw in the last chapter, we wake up to the dimension of depth most vividly when the bottom falls out of our lives in one way or another. And so it is with the future. It is when we suffer the imprisonment by our past that we begin to attend more directly to the reality of the future. When the past looms so large in our experience as almost to exclude the entrance of a fresh future, then the future becomes of interest. Concern for our being is awakened most intensely in the presence of the threat of non-being. The desire for truth is aroused most decisively after the disappointing encounter with falsehood. The experience of one's chains, it has been said, is the first step toward an appreciation of freedom. Beauty stands out more prominently after we have experienced ugliness. We might also say that it is especially the sense of imprisonment in one's past that awakens one's concern for the future.

Our question "What is the future?" cannot be an interesting one unless we have first felt the confinement of the past. But there is a paradox here. For we cannot feel the past as confining unless in some mode of present experience we have already felt the future. To know a limit *as a limit* is already to be beyond that limit. To recognize the past truly as past means that we already have some vague sense of futurity. The future, even when it seems to be absent, has already quietly insinuated itself into our present subjective awareness. By comparison with the silent horizon of this future our past shows up in awareness precisely as pastness.

If the future has already inserted itself into our present, perhaps we may begin to feel a troubling conflict. This conflict involves a struggle between the urge to secure our existence in the settled sureness of the past on the one hand, and the desire to open ourselves to the surprisingness of a fresh future on the other. As I have been emphasizing, the encroachment of the future into the present is an objective, undeniable given. We have calendars and clocks to prove it. But, *subjectively* speaking, we may relate to this ingression of the future in different modes of awareness and being. Our subjective openness to the future seldom coincides with the objective fact of futurity. Typically our response to its inevitable coming is one of at least partial denial. To a great extent we anxiously resist the entrance of novelty and freshness into our experience. In the previous chapter we noticed how we turn our lives away from any intense encounter with depth until the depth itself carries us into its abysmal and grounding embrace. Here I would add that our meeting with the future has a similar structure.

As with depth, the future is fundamentally a *mysterium tremendum et fascinans*. It evokes in us ambivalent responses. We may, and often do, shrink back from it as an awesome and overwhelming terror, as a *mysterium tremendum*. We feel, with some reason, that it will loosen us from our moorings to the safety of the past. This severance may be a difficult one, depending on the degree to which we have made the past or present normative for our life. But the future is also a *mysterium fascinans*, compellingly attractive and promising a fulfillment not yet attained. There is something in us that longs for the future to deliver us from the decay of the past and the boredom of the present. We intuit a healing power in the future. We form images of it in our daydreams, in our symbols, myths, utopias and in our religions. But, as with the dimension of depth, our relationship to the future is ambiguous. The future is both the object of our deepest longing and at the same time an horizon that we would like to recede into a less threatening distance. We would make the past or present the absolute criterion of our lives rather than allow ourselves to be carried away into the unfamiliar freshness of the future.

Our native openness to the future is usually awakened most intensely in those moments of our life and in periods of human history when the past or present seems insufficient to nurture our longings. This is why a sense of the future takes root most firmly among the oppressed. The reaching out for something radically new does not easily occur in the midst of ease and satisfaction with the status quo. Often it is only when the resources of the past and present have been spent that we begin to open ourselves willingly to the future.

And yet the presence of the future may also be felt even in the midst of satiety. After reaching a long sought goal, after achieving a coveted status, after having our dreams realized, we begin to feel an unanticipated emptiness when the initial joy of accomplishment has begun to fade. We experience what the great philosopher of the future, Ernst Bloch, has called the "melancholy of fulfillment." We continue to long for something new because of our innate capacity for receiving more and more of the future. Psychology speaks of the "success syndrome," or at times of the "wrecked by success syndrome." Having arrived at the goal of an ardent desire, we renounce the enjoyment of its attainment. So in order to avoid the open-

ended future that confronts us as a void, we pause at the
doorway of success and turn back. Perhaps there is something unhealthy about our shrinking back from any particular success, but there may also be an underlying intuition
that no particular achievement will bring us ultimate satisfaction. With Nietzsche we may prefer to be saved "from
all petty victories." There is an intimation that only the
future, in its utter inexhaustibility, will be able to fill us up.

The future can be both beckoning and terrifying. We
long for it and are repelled by it. We need it, and we try to
avoid it. It is inexorable, and yet we try to prevent its happening. At times, however, we may be forced by circumstances to release our hold on the past and to accept the
indeterminacy of the future. To our surprise often (and we
might even say *always*, if we wait long enough in patience)
it turns out that the future brings us what we really longed
for at levels of desire to which we previously had not
adverted. As in the case of depth, the future is not only an
abyss from which we understandably recoil; it is also a
ground that promises ultimate fulfillment.

However, not just any particular future is capable of
satisfying us. Even if it happens that we arrive at an imag-
ined "utopia" in our individual or social life, we inevitably
find that it too will be relativized by the horizon of a future
beyond itself. It will be exposed as finite and fragile, and we
will have to continue our quest. Each particular future is relative, and so it turns out to be too narrow to appease the
deep hunger for the future that constitutes the dynamism
of human and social life. It is apparent that we never arrive
completely at the future we long for, and that if we momentarily think we have arrived, we are soon disappointed. It
may be tempting for some of us then to interpret the future
as an infinite void with no ultimate ground, and to see our
lives as futile forays into this infinite emptiness. The ever

receding character of the future may seem to make despair the most honest attitude we can take toward it. More than one philosopher has taken this position.

And yet only a brief glance at the generality of human experience shows us that for the most part we pick up the pieces of our shattered dreams and hopefully renew our quest after having experienced the disappointments in each particular future. We still attempt to transcend the relativity of our particular futures. We are driven by the hope for an *absolute future*.[1] Is such a hope completely deluded? Or are the philosophers of despair the ones who hold the truth?

Whether the quest for an *absolute* future, one that does not ultimately disappoint, is a philosophically "realistic" undertaking for us is a question that will be dealt with later in this chapter (and again in Chapter 5). For now, however, let us be content with a simple reflection on our own experience of the particular futures we have hoped for and been disappointed by. Notice especially how a margin of unfulfilled longing inserts itself and then continues to grow after you have achieved some goal or been surprised by some special happening in your life. Note the restlessness that sets in, and which you may initially repress, but which then grows more and more annoying until you have to pay attention to it. It is as though it were saying: "Your future still lies before you. Do not rest yet. You are capable of growing indefinitely into the inexhaustible future that stretches out before you." If you have ever had such an experience of the threatening and promising future you are in a position to understand the meaning of the word "God."

The name of this infinite and inexhaustible future is God. That future is what the word God means. And if that word has not much meaning for you, translate it, and speak of your ultimate future, of what you hope for in the depths of your desire. Perhaps in order to do this, you must forget many things that you have learned about God, perhaps even that word itself. For if you know that God means the *absolute future,* you know much about the divine. You cannot then call yourself an atheist or unbeliever. For you cannot think or say: Life has no future! Reality lies only in the past! The present is sufficient! For whoever has a concern about the absolute future is concerned about God.[2]

Here I have substituted the word "future" for depth because the metaphor "depth" is only partly able to illuminate what many people mean by God (as Tillich himself was no doubt aware). What is signified by the term "God" is only fragmentarily conceptualized by reference to the dimension of depth. Such reference in fact is meant to be only a starting point, one that leaves us with further questions concerning the "location" of the divine. The advantage of the "depth" metaphor is that it is capable of illuminating religious experience in a cross-cultural manner. It can integrate the religious experience of Asians with that of the West, of North American Indians with Australian aborigines, of Eskimos with Africans. Moreover, a common concern for depth may put the atheist in the same camp as the mystic, the theist with the secular humanist. A common concern for moving away from mediocrity and superficiality is, after all, more significant than the explicit symbolic differences that divide sects and ideologies on the surface of language. The advantage of reference to the dimension of depth is that it points to common elements in the spiritual, moral, intellectual, aesthetic and political life of cultures and individuals whose explicit teachings may be incompatible with one another. And it contains an implicit criterion whereby we might evaluate various points of view: the measure of their genuineness, their truth and their value is the degree of concern for depth that they manifest. For example, an atheist who in his or her life lives with a passionate concern for justice, peace or compassion is obviously more intimate with the depth (that is, with what we are calling God) than is the theist whose beliefs are employed as part of the ideological justification of an inequitable economic order. Thus thinking of the dimension of depth is one important way of thinking about God.

And yet the "depth" metaphor is by itself inadequate in pointing to the reality of what people understand by God. It needs to be complemented by other ideas. Among these is that of *futurity*. Particularly in biblical religion the idea of God is inseparable from our experience of the future. The Bible may even be said to have opened up our consciousness to a radically new way of experiencing the depth of reality, namely as essentially future.[3] Even today's secular experience of the future has been influenced by the biblical location of God's reality in the dimension of futurity. This "eschatological" sense that the "really real" world lies up ahead in the future is shared by Marxists and capitalist consumer cultures alike, even though they may either explicitly or implicitly deny the existence of God. Ironically this secularistic way of experiencing the future is an indirect descendant of the biblical optimism according to which God heals and addresses people in history out of an ever-receding future. The idea of God has dropped out of the picture, but the future orientation has remained alive in many non-religious movements, often more vigorously than in theistic settings. Today's biblical scholarship has shown clearly that the ancient Hebrew religious experience differed from that of its contemporaries essentially in its loosening the sacred from its bondage to the circularity of nature's seasons and placing it in the realm of the indefinite historical future. And the central challenge for the early devotees of the biblical Yahweh was to forsake the safety of a purely nature-oriented religion and surrender them-

selves to the uncertainty of living in a history whose promise seemed to lie far off in the future. We in the West are all
heirs to this dramatic rupture of history and nature, even if
we no longer have any explicit religious beliefs. But we are
also heirs to the ancient temptation to despair of history's
promise and to take refuge in one or other of the many ideological, pharmacological, political or cultural avenues for
escaping it. For some the way to "happiness" is simply that
of merging once again with nature and forsaking the "ter-
rors of history." For others, however, there is no turning
back. The way to the depth requires an openness to the
dimension of historical futurity with all of the patient waiting "in joyful expectation" that this posture demands.

If our emphasizing the future in this way seems to
downgrade the importance of the past and of tradition, then
this impression must be corrected. Openness to the future
is the very condition of, and not an obstacle to, recovering
the meaning of the past and of the important traditions of
our human history. The horizon of the future liberates significant events and traditions from the heaviness of merely
having been and opens up a space in which they can come
to life once again.

It has been observed that a radical contemporaneity
which ignores the past is the first step toward barbarism.[4]
Were we to forget the eons of human effort and suffering
that have given poignancy and depth to the symbols and
myths in the great traditions we would be hurled into a cultural and ethical vacuum. We have an obligation to keep
these traditions alive, to come to know their meaning more
and more intimately. One of the failings of Western thought
since the Enlightenment has been its cavalier assumption
that ancient traditions have little if anything to teach us. In
its legitimate questioning of the suffocating effects of

"authority" untutored by experience and reason it may have gone too far in overlooking the wisdom buried in the traditional teachings. In this sense, at least, "modernity" has deserved the suspicion of its recent critics. But to hold that the past has something to teach us is not to insist that we have to return to the past and forget the gains of modernity. Neither does it mean that the past is more significant than the future. There is no way we can escape the pressure of the future, any more than we can eliminate the depth beneath the surface of our existence. What we can do is approach this future in a spirit of hope and courage communicated by the wisdom of great women and men of the past. Openness to the future should never occur at the expense of forgetting the suffering of forgotten peoples of the past or the wisdom molded by tragedy that has been deposited in the great teachings of our traditions. But these traditions are intended to instruct us, not to enslave us.

Another way to think about God, then, is as the absolute future. God is not an object of our experience so much as a *dimension* or *horizon* of our experience. Not all things that are real are potential objects of human experience. The dimension of futurity, as of depth, is certainly real, without thereby being subject to our intellectual or perceptual mastery. Perhaps, therefore, God may be understood less as a potential *object* of experience than as a dimension, condition and future horizon of all our experience.

And as the *absolute* future "God" means the irrepressible promise of fulfillment that emerges anew out of the infinite (and seemingly empty) horizon of our future each time we experience disappointment. "God" means the ground of hope that animates us to search further whenever we realize that we have not yet arrived at what we really long for.

The Absence of God

Locating God's presence in the arena of the future can help us to understand the apparent absence of God. Scientifically oriented philosophers usually challenge theists to show some present evidence of God's reality. They seek something in the manner of a positive, scientific demonstration of God's *objective* contemporary existence. And when theists fail to adduce such verification they are accused of fostering an illusion, that is, of being unrealistic. The existence of that which is said to be of ultimate importance is not even as obvious as that of a rock. How can the intelligent, scientifically enlightened person seriously believe in God?

Our answer to this question is simply that the scientific, empirical approach is oriented toward a region of reality, the present, that is insufficiently expansive to contain the reality of God. We may think of the appropriate region of God's reality as essentially the future (although also embracing the past and present).[5] Understood as the absolute future the reality of God lies beyond the limits of what can be grasped in the present. The methods we employ in understanding the present are inadequate for orienting us to the future. Science is fixed on the present or past, and it is incapable of dealing with the future since there is no way it can bring the dimension of the yet-to-come under any sort of verificational control. Only imagination suffused with hope can bring the future within view. The reality of God, therefore, must be approached in the same general way as we approach any aspect of the future, namely by hoping and imagining.

Of course the empiricist will object that future-oriented imagination is a mere extrapolation from our present wishes, that our longing for the future and picturing it symbolically may have nothing to do with "reality." However, this objection applies more to wishing than to hoping, and we must carefully distinguish between these two postures. Hoping is an openness to the breaking in of what is radically new and unanticipated.[6] Wishing, on the other hand, is the illusory extension into the future of what we want at the present moment. Wishing is not an openness to the future but is oriented entirely from the present. In order to hope, on the other hand, we need to relativize our wishing and open ourselves to the prospect of being surprised by the radically new. Such an attitude requires a courageous asceticism of its own, a painful renunciation of our tendency to cling obsessively to the present or past. Hoping is not an escape from reality, nor is it as easy as its critics insist.[7] Hoping is an attitude capable of living tolerantly with the absence of God.

Religion

If the ultimate environment of our lives is not only depth, but also the absolute future, then we must understand "religion" accordingly. We may say, then, that religion is not only concern for depth or the expression in symbol and ritual of a shared sense of depth. Without denying any of this we must now add that in connection with the horizon of an absolute future religion is essentially *hope*.[8]

We must be careful to distinguish hope from other forms of desire. It may be very tempting to follow the suggestion of Freud that religion is nothing other than a product of the pleasure principle, that religion is an illusion created by an intense desire to escape "reality" and to merge in an infantile manner with maternal nature or a paternal God who would satisfy our hunger for gratification. We need not deny that there might be something to what Freud has to say here about the nature of human desire. But if we understand the idea of God as that which challenges us to open ourselves radically to the future, we must distinguish what we are calling religion from Freud's position. After all, in Freud's critique religion is always understood as a regressive tendency, as a hankering for a lost love-object from one's *past* psychic experience. This obsession with the idol of the past is the very temptation that biblical religion itself disowned, especially in the prophetic strains of that tradition. The Hebrew prophets would themselves have agreed with Freud that we humans are able to do better than simply spend our lives attempting to recover a lost parental love. They might even have concurred with psychoanalysis that many of our portraits of God are inevitably overlaid with regressive images of frustrated relations to significant others in our psychic history. But they would have insisted beyond this that the place of encounter with God is in hope for a radically new future rather than in nostalgia for past safeties. They would look back to the past not to retrieve it as past, but to find there precedents for looking forward to the surprising action of God in their future.[9]

The heart of religion, in this context at least, may be thought of as hope for an "absolute future." Such hope is not a renunciation of the reality principle if it turns out that the substance of reality lies in the future rather than in the present or the past. There is no evidence that the present and the past exhaust the limits of reality. It may be that the "really real" lies up ahead, and that our historical existence is only a fragmentary and inadequate anticipation of this future. Our anticipation of the fullness of reality would then take the form of *imagining* the future in such a way as to allow for its entrance into the present. A certain kind of adventurous dreaming would be the way in which we would follow the Freudian imperative to "face reality." A failure to construct creative visions that motivate us to action that would usher in the future would be a refusal to be realistic. And if the fullness of God's being is essentially future, then realistic religion consists in the hopeful and imaginative quest for this future.

As soon as we connect the origin of the idea of God in any way to human imagination, however, it seems that we have undermined the credibility to thought of any reference to the divine. For the imagination is considered by many thinkers to be an untrustworthy faculty whose favorite pastime is the spinning of illusions. Imagination is held to be uninterested in reality and totally in the service of the pleasure principle. To state that imagination conditions our thinking about God seems to be an admission of the illusory nature of the idea of God. Psychologically speaking, "God" seems to be nothing more than a *projection.*

The projection theory of religion accounts for the origin of the "sense of God" by locating it in human wishing. According to the projection theory the intensity of our passion for God is sufficient to explain the vividness and palpability of our impression that we are "in fact" encompassed by a divine reality. And the anthropomorphic characteristics with which we clothe our deities seem to be conclusive evidence that "God" is nothing more than the projection of our own personal attributes onto a chimera invented by our wishing. Though he was not himself an "atheist," the ancient Greek philosopher Xenophanes (sixth century B.C.) surmised that " . . . if cattle and horses had hands, or were able to draw and do the works that men can do, horses would draw the forms of the gods like horses, and cattle like cattle, and they would make their bodies such as they each had themselves." And this suspicion of projection in religion was shared by several other ancient philosophers and more recently by enlightenment thinkers like Voltaire who quipped that "man creates God in his own image and likeness." (Mark Twain, somewhat more humorously, put it as follows: "God created man in his own image, and man, being a gentleman, returned the compliment.")

Since the nineteenth century, however, these formerly scattered misgivings about the origin of the sense of God have given way to a torrent of suspicion that claims a place of great prominence in modern thought. The names of Friedrich Nietzsche, Ludwig Feuerbach, Karl Marx, Emile Durkheim and Sigmund Freud are all associated with the suspicion that human projective imagining is the exclusive origin of our impression of the divine. And the countless intellectuals and academics who have adopted one or other form of the projection theory make it impossible for us either to ignore the suspicion that religion is mere projection or to withhold some response to this significant theory.

How, then, is the thoughtful believer to respond to the almost timeless suspicion that "the divine" is nothing more than a projection? And if there is indeed an element of projection in religion, does this fact alone invalidate the idea of the divine?

In the first place, if the "location" of the divine is as the "horizon" of our experience, as I have suggested, then we may ask how we could relate to it without some aspect of projection. Since, by definition, we cannot embrace or objectify the horizon of depth or futurity, how are we to speak of it at all without representing it in terms of concrete images derived from our experience of objects, events or persons that are encompassed by this horizon? In other words, how are we to avoid "symbolic" reference to the divine, which by its very nature requires the use of images? Furthermore, if this horizon is of paramount importance to us, why would we not represent it in terms of images of those realities from our immediate environment that are most significant to us, namely human personalities? Therefore, should we be altogether embarrassed if our sense of the divine is overlaid with images of paternity or maternity or with attributes such as intelligence, will, and affectivity? Those who are truly religious do not take such images literally anyway, since it is essential to religion that we keep constantly before us a sense of the infinite distance between the divine and our representations thereof. Furthermore, religion is essentially open to revision of its images since it realizes that no particular symbolic representation of ultimacy fully contains the horizon of depth or futurity pointed to and mediated to our finite consciousness by way of the imaginative symbols and stories of religious traditions.

But the question persists. Where does our sense of God come from? It seems on the surface that there are only two conceivable answers to this most important question: *either* it comes from God by way of some kind of direct revelation, *or* it emanates from us human beings who by force of our imaginations have ourselves created the powerful impression of God's reality out of what is in fact an illusion. These two positions initially seem to exhaust the possible answers, and the projection theory rules out the first as incapable of scientific verification. However, there is a third option that we may also entertain: it is possible in principle that if God is really God, namely, transcendent and ultimate in being, then both of the above alternatives can be combined into a single, and more plausible, "hypothesis" concerning the origin of our "sense of God." It is possible that the origin of our sense of God may be explained in part as the product of our desire while at the same time being explained also as the result of our consciousness being taken hold of by the actuality of the divine. Both imagina-

tive human longing and divine reality may together constitute our sense of God.

The British scholar of religion, John Bowker, even
insists that if God is a reality it would be surprising not to
find a great deal of projection and illusion in concrete religious life. In other words, it is plausible to hold that the
very reality of the divine has aroused our desire for God in
the first place, and that in response to this arousal we stum-
ble to meet the evasive divine horizon loaded with "projected" images which seem, psychologically speaking, to be
nothing but illusions. However, Bowker says,

> . . . it would be impossible on psychoanalytic grounds
> alone to exclude the possibility that God is a source of
> the sense of God: however much a sense of God may
> be constructed through, and as a consequence of infan-
> tile experience, and however much the characterization
> of God may replicate parental relationships, the possi-
> bility cannot be excluded that there may be x in reality
> which has in the past sustained those replications and
> which has reinforced the continuity of such terms as
> 'God'.[10]

According to this third, more comprehensive, "hypothesis" it is the very ultimacy and transcendence of God that
would explain the "scandal" of religion's lack of stability
throughout the ages. The birth and death of countless deities, the ironically shifting and evanescent nature of the
symbolic representations of an allegedly eternal absolute,
has made historical religions appear to their critics as fickle
and foundationless. One would expect that if there were
any substance to these religions they would be more resis-
tant to the erosions of time. If they were trustworthy indi-
cators of a veritable divine revelation they should have

more durability to them. As H. L. Mencken put it in his blunt "burial service" for the gods:

> Where is the grave-yard of dead gods? What lingering mourner waters their mounds? . . . Men labored for generations to build vast temples to them—temples with stones as large as hay-wagons. The business of interpreting their whims occupied thousands of priests, wizards, archdeacons, evangelists, haruspices, bishops, archbishops. To doubt them was to die, usually at the stake. Armies took to the fields to defend them against infidels: villages were burned, women and children were butchered, cattle were driven off. . . . They were gods of the highest standing and dignity—gods of civilized peoples—worshipped and believed in by millions. All were theoretically omnipotent, omniscient and immortal. And all are dead.[11]

To the skeptic the eventual displacement of religious images is proof of their unreliability. To Bowker, however, the instability of religious life and consciousness is just what we should expect if the divine is indeed a reality. Because of its eminence and transcendence no particular representation of the divine could adequately encapsulate it. And the religious sense of this symbolic inadequacy would be expressed in a reluctance to take particular images of God with unreserved seriousness. Religion would be open to an iconoclasm undertaken in the interest of finding fuller and more faithful replicas of the divine. Then births and burials of gods would be intelligible as part of the ageless and never ending quest for the absolute.

I would add to Bowker's ideas the suggestion that his position is also tolerant of the "apophatic" moments in religious history (such as Theravada Buddhism and other "mystical" forms of religion) where great visionaries have

grown altogether weary of images because of their inevitable inadequacy, and have advocated a serene silence with
respect to the absolute. At the same time, however, it is not
surprising that the imaginative quest for the divine period-
ically arises anew for those to whom absolute silence about
the divine is not humanly satisfying. Religious experimen-
tation with lively symbols and stories may be necessary to
bring the sense of God into layers of our consciousness that
are not appeased by a purely "negative" theology.

A useful analogy from our human experience may help
us understand how necessary our projections are in any
possible encounter with the divine, even if these projections
possess an aspect of illusion.[12] When a young man falls in
love with a young woman it is not unusual that the first
stage of the romantic involvement is overlaid with illusory
expectations. Thus the young man will project onto his
beloved an exaggerated aura of tenderness and perhaps
perfect femininity that the young woman in fact cannot live
up to. And so if the relationship is to continue he must
revise his illusions, though he may never completely abandon them. The story of the relationship as it develops is one
of continual revisions of illusions so as more closely to
approach the reality of the other person. This process will
involve moments of painful disillusionment as well as the
satisfaction of seeing more deeply into the reality of the
other. The point is that, while epistemologically suspect,
the romantic illusions seem to be inevitable developmental
stages in the young man's encounter with the beloved.

The case may be similar in the story of humanity's
quest of and encounter with the divine, understood as the
absolute future. As we humans have searched for the ultimate objective of our desire it is not surprising that the initial phase of longing would have a strong aspect of childish
wishing and that, therefore, our religions would always be

accompanied by at least some degree of projection. And while the philosopher of religion is rightly intolerant of this infantilism, the historian or psychologist can be more understanding and may even locate the illusions of religion as "necessary" developmental stages in our search for the reality of God. And I would add that if the dimension of futurity is appropriate for our "locating" the reality of God, then the "unavailability" or constantly receding nature of this horizon demands that our imaginations continually revise our "sense" of it. Such creative, imaginative representation of the dimension of futurity is not simply illusory but is instead the only way by which in the present the dimension of the absolute future can take hold of us. Were we to cease visionary dreaming altogether we would cut ourselves off from the divine. And if there is an element of wishing that always adheres to our images of hope, then we should try as far as possible to purify our hope of such infantile and illusory desire. But the persistence in our actual religious life of immature levels of desire, which are the levels most available to psychological analysis, does not all by itself warrant a reduction of all religion to an archaic pining for an irrecoverable past. In its essence religion seeks a transcendence of such archaism by opening itself imaginatively to the instability of living within the horizon of an absolute future.

At the risk of oversimplification we may refer to those "religious" attitudes that renounce hope in the future and seek to escape history by elevating a past or present cultural ideal into a timeless eternity as "gnosticism." It has been pointed out that gnostic forms of religion often originate among social groups that have been divested of an elite cultural or socio-political status.[13] Sensing the impossibility of their ever recovering an exalted status again on the plain of history, gnostics attempt to establish for themselves a privileged status on the trans-temporal plain of eternity. They think of themselves as privy to a secret knowledge or "gnosis" that makes them special in the eyes of God, and they erect obstacles in the form of sometimes impossible initiation rites as a condition for others' entering into the exceptional circle of gnosis.

This kind of religiosity seems to be the result of a temptation to escape the messiness of historical existence and openness to the future by rising imaginatively above the sphere of temporality altogether.[14] Much that passes as religion (and philosophy as well) falls within this broadly, and certainly inadequately defined phenomenon that I am calling gnosticism. But precisely because of its escapist attitude and its aversion to the dimension of futurity, it has earned the suspicion of future-oriented religion, that is of "eschatologically" influenced religious traditions. The danger of taking the "depth" metaphor too one-sidedly is that it might appeal to the gnostic tendency to move vertically outside of the realm of our historicity. For that reason many of us would insist that an understanding of religion as the quest for depth includes as its inner substance a radical openness to the absolute future. This future comes to meet us in the hopeful images that arise out of our existing in concrete history, but it does not demand that we abandon this history in order to escape into a timeless eternity. Instead it invites us to transform our historical existence, as far as we are humanly able to do so, into the shape of the hopeful images through which the depth of the future discloses itself to us.

Chapter 3
Freedom

Very few words evoke as much positive sentiment as "freedom." At the same time very few words are more difficult to define. Politicians, philosophers, psychologists and theologians have all discussed the term. And yet, after hearing what they have to say about it, we are still left with the question: What exactly is freedom? One is tempted to paraphrase St. Augustine's famous lament about his inability to spell out the meaning of time: If no one asks me what freedom is then I know what it is; but if someone asks me, then I do not know. Freedom can be rendered intuitively vivid through symbols, myths and stories of heroic struggles for "emancipation" or "liberation." And the sense of freedom is concretized in actually living and acting rather than by reading or writing a book. Any conceptual or theoretical attempt to say what freedom is risks becoming shallow and abstract, and there is a good chance that it will partially warp our immediate grasp of the meaning of the term. Nonetheless, perhaps some insight can be gained from a theoretical study of the idea of freedom. And just as Augustine after all could not refrain from telling us what time is, so it is forgivable if we also attempt to speak conceptually about freedom. We know the extent to which ideas have contributed to the formation of our history. Certainly our experience of freedom in the Western world has been shaped significantly by bold ideas that in turn motivated people to work for liberation from various forms of oppression. It is not entirely out of place, therefore, to discuss the *idea* of freedom in a theoretical way.

What, then, is freedom? As in our intuition of time we all have an immediate or "naive" grasp of the meaning of "freedom." The same is true of our experience of depth and futurity. We feel them, we dwell in them, and we sense their presence or absence in various degrees. But we cannot objectify them. We cannot hold them out before us in a controlling fashion such as science attempts to do with the objects of its study. We know them more in the mode of being grasped by them than by actually grasping them ourselves. Or we know them in the mode of fleeing from them. The same is also true of our understanding of freedom. We know what it is only if we have been grasped by it or, in a negative sense, if we have fled from it. If we try to lay hold of it ourselves it slips away from us. Our approach to it must therefore be somewhat indirect, and we should not expect ever to have a perfectly clear intellectual grasp of what it is.

There are three ways in which philosophers have typically dealt with the notion of freedom. One way is to understand freedom as something we have, another as something we are, and yet another as something that has us. The first approach views freedom as one of our faculties, the one whereby we make "free choices" among various alternatives that are offered to us. The ability to make free choices is certainly an important aspect of freedom but free choice is not coextensive with freedom as we shall understand it here. The second approach, exemplified in an extreme way by the French philosopher Jean-Paul Sartre, views freedom as the very essence of human existence. In this view human reality *is* freedom, in the negative sense of not being determined by anything beyond itself and, in the positive sense, as the creative source of our very identities.[1] This position that we *are* freedom would be acceptable if we understood freedom as finite and not as absolute in the sense given by Sartre. To say that we are finite freedom is one important way to understand our nature. However, even this second meaning does not give us the depth toward which the word freedom points. For that reason I shall dwell hereafter on a third meaning of the term. Freedom in the deepest sense is something that takes hold of us, and not something that we can manipulate ourselves. Moreover, we owe our freedom to choose (freedom in the first sense) as well as the freedom of our finite existence (freedom in the second sense) to our participating in the encompassing freedom (in the third sense) of which I shall speak in the present chapter. Freedom in the third and most substantive sense is the "ground" of freedom in the first two instances.[2]

If we reflect on some very obvious aspects of our experience, as we have done in the previous two chapters, we shall observe that freedom is most appropriately understood as the comprehensive *horizon* of our existence rather than as something we possess or, as Jean-Paul Sartre has proposed, something that coincides with our individual existence. As in the case of depth and futurity, freedom, in the sense of something that grasps us, is a *mysterium tremendum et fascinans.* We shrink from it in fear that we will be lost in its embrace, and at the same time we long for it passionately, intuiting that our personal fulfillment consists of our eventually surrendering to it. We long for the freedom that coincides with our absolute future, but at the same time we are reluctant to allow it into our present life.

In order to illustrate concretely the ambivalence of our relationship to freedom let us look especially at the experience of coming to grips with our own personal identities. Have there been times when we came up to the point of knowing that we really are not fully definable in terms of our immediate surroundings? Have we on some occasions realized that the opinion others have of us simply does not adequately indicate what we know ourselves to be? Such moments hold open to us the possibility of our entering into a whole new way of existing, and yet we usually revert to the typical routine of allowing past patterns of others' expectations to determine how we view ourselves. Psychoanalysis, though controversial in many respects, at least deserves our admiration for showing us how our early family life unconsciously accompanies us and shapes our attitudes throughout our lives. Many of us can go through an entire lifetime without ever questioning the familial patterns of expectation that gave us our earliest orientation in the world. Because of the power and authority of these familial patterns, any attempt we make at alternative self-definition may be accompanied by an agonizing sense of guilt and betrayal.

It is instructive to examine the sense of uneasiness that often accompanies the act of departing from the expectations that we think others have imposed upon us. At times such a departure is, of course, the violation of standards that we are expected to model ourselves on as the basic minimum for human existence. In such a case genuine feelings of guilt are important to point out to us the error of our ways and to goad us into conforming to the cardinal standards of human conduct. But at other times we need to "violate" certain conventional standards if we think they are an obstacle to the realization of genuine new possibilities of being human to which we sincerely feel called. But we are uneasy before these possibilities as well. It is much easier to be merely conventional in our ethical life than to heed the summons of timeless values that transcend our societal, national or familial ideals.[3]

We may call this sense of dread in the face of new possibilities "anxiety." One meaning of "anxiety" is the awareness of yet unrealized possibilities. It is the intimation that we have other routes of self-definition open to us alongside those that have been so determinative in the past. Our awareness of these unrealized possibilities that would give a new cast to our identity confronts us as a *tremendum*. Unlike the realm of the "actual" the arena of the "possible" is inexhaustible, and so we are reluctant to plunge into its formless, abysmal depths, dreading that the boundaries of our finite existence will be annihilated by the excess of the possible. As Kierkegaard puts it, our impression of this realm of sheer unrealized possibility may induce in us a "sickness unto death."[4] However, one aspect of the experience of freedom consists precisely of the anxiety evoked in us by our awareness of ever new possibilities, ideals or values.

An analysis of this anxiety can open us to a deeper understanding of freedom. When we use the term anxiety here, though, we are not referring to something abnormal or pathological. Rather we are talking about a state of awareness that always accompanies our human existence whether in a conscious or in an unconscious way. Without it we would not be human existents at all. In other words, this anxiety is a characteristic aspect or our existence, and not something that can be removed pharmacologically or psychiatrically. When psychiatry talks about removing anxiety it is speaking of a pathological exaggeration or suppression of our "normal" anxiety. And it seriously misleads us if it pretends to cure us of our "existential" anxiety.[5] Nothing can cure us of this anxiety. But such an impossibility need not be the occasion of perpetual unhappiness for us. Instead it may be seen as an opening to the fulfilling side of freedom.

Existential anxiety may also be understood as the awareness of the fact that our existence is constantly subject to a fundamental and unavoidable threat. Paul Tillich refers to it as the threat of "non-being."[6] The awareness of this threat should be distinguished from fear.[7] Fear is always a response to a specific danger, to a definite object of terror. For example, I may fear a rabid animal, an authoritarian teacher, a poor grade on an examination, or the disapproval of parents and friends. And I may combat my fear of these by employing specific strategies. I may shoot the rabid animal, change classes to a more amiable instructor, study harder for an examination, or move away from home. Such strategies are often successful ways of coping with fear. Yet beneath all our specific fears there is a sustained inkling of a pervasive and ineradicable threat which no evasive action can alleviate. There is at least a vague intuition that our existence is situated precariously over against the threat of "non-being."

Some philosophers object to the usage of so difficult a notion as "non-being." They assert, somewhat simplistically, that if something is non-being then it cannot be talked about at all, and that reference to it is nonsense. The fact that "non-being" sounds so slippery and appears so indefinable, however, is not surprising once we look into it. There is a reason why we cannot clearly lay hold of this notion. This non-being is an aspect of the *horizon* of our existence, and it corresponds with what we called the "abysmal" aspect of depth in our first chapter. If the reader has difficulty with the term "non-being" I would suggest that he or she simply think of what we referred to as the experience of the "abyss" which usually precedes a deeper sense of being grounded. It manifests itself most obviously in our sense of the fact that we are never in complete control of our lives, that there is always the element of *fate* which interferes with our projects. I may undertake numerous evasive strategies to eliminate fear, but I will still find that "something" deeper and more intransigent than any specific object of fear lurks beneath the surface of my life and will not go away. This "something" may be called non-being because it persists as a threat to my "being."

My life never turns out exactly the way I planned it. I can never totally eliminate fate. And the absolute limit to any control I have over my life is made evident in my awareness that I must eventually die. The threat of non-being is perhaps most obvious in the fact of having-to-die. Thus if we tie the notion of "non-being" to the experience we all have of our fatedness and of our having-to-die, then it takes on a "substantiality" that renders it a legitimate and meaningful notion, though admittedly it lacks the clarity that pertains to more trivial objects of experience.

We may also use the term "non-being" because we need some broader and more inclusive notion than either fate or death to name that "something" that continually threatens our existence. For fate and death do not exhaust this threat. There are also the threats of guilt and self-rejection which in a sense are even more potent than fate and death.[8] Our existence, as we noted earlier, is always capable of realizing new possibilities. It is not stuck in one static identity indefinitely. And yet it always falls short of realizing the possibilities open to it. For example, there may be a part of me that would make a good doctor, another part a

good student, teacher, social worker, politician, or simply a
better, more caring person. Concretely I will not be able to
realize all such possibilities. Every concrete decision that I
make means that I am cutting myself off from *(de-cidere)* an
inexhaustible number of alternative possibilities in order to
realize this particular one. The gap between what I am and
what I could be is felt as *guilt*. Again, this anxiety of guilt is
not a pathological but a normal state of finite human existence. Without it I could scarcely be called human. What
distinguishes human existence from that of mere objects is
that the former is capable of imagining ever new possibilities for itself which set up a tension between present actuality and alternative possibility. The awareness of this tension
is not unhealthy but is the condition for moving toward the
realization of at least some of one's genuine possibilities.

Thus there is a healthy or animating sense of guilt,
understood as the awareness that one has not realized one's
realistic possibilities. However, if the word "guilt" is understood as the crippling self-rejection that accompanies a
sense of failure to attain *unrealistic* goals, then it may take
on a pathological status. The obsession with unrealistic
goals can become an imprisoning experience that intensifies
our ordinary fatedness to the point of rendering it unbear-
able. The problem of human existence then becomes not
only that of finding strength to accept our fatedness and
mortality, but, even more, that of accepting our lives as subject to the threat of guilt and self-rejection. Thus the threat
of non-being goes beyond what Tillich calls the "ontic"
threats of fate and death and also includes the "moral"
threats of guilt and self-rejection.

As if such threats were not enough, it also happens that
those ingredients of culture (its traditions, myths, symbols
and art) that do give us strength to face the anxiety of fate,
death and guilt sometimes lose their capacity to enliven us,

become subject to criticism, and leave us in doubt about the very meaning of our existence. When such symbols lose their power over our consciousness we may be tempted to despair of finding any meaning at all. Much so-called "existentialist" literature and art has depicted this sense of despair in the present century. It emphasizes that non-being is felt by many today most intensely in the "spiritual" threats of doubt and meaninglessness rather than simply in the experience of fate, death and guilt. Without meaning human existence hovers even more obviously over the abyss of non-being.

In summary, then, non-being threatens us ontically in the form of fate and death, morally in the form of guilt and the sense of being condemned or rejected, and spiritually in the form of emptiness (or doubt) and meaninglessness.[9]

But what does this discussion of non-being have to do with freedom? Strange as it may initially seem, the experience of the threat of non-being that I have just described (drawing again from Paul Tillich) is one aspect of the experience of the horizon of freedom. "Non-being" is the face that freedom first presents to us as it invites us into its embrace. And difficult as it may be for us to understand, it is by realistically facing rather than running away from this non-being that we are liberated from the things that enslave us and drawn toward the fullness of freedom.

Non-being is terrifying to us, of course, and so we attempt to avoid it by tying our fragile existence to things that seemingly provide refuge from it. However, since all such things are themselves merely finite and therefore subject to non-being also, the security they give us is only fragmentary and ultimately illusory. Such precarious security is not truly liberating in the final analysis, for it merely constricts our lives by binding us to objects that are too small to help us face existential anxiety. Just as we strive to turn the anxiety of non-being into specific objects of fear that we can control, so also we turn to specific objects, persons, events, nations, cults, possessions, etc., in order to anchor our existence against the invasion of non-being. Eventually, however, we will be forced to realize that they are mere "idols" that cannot give us the ultimate deliverance for which we really hope. How, then, are we to deal with non-being?

The threat of non-being can be met adequately only by a courage proportionate to the threat itself.[10] It is through *courage* that we meet the threat of non-being, and in doing so experience freedom-itself. Indeed, courage may be defined as the "self-affirmation" by which we accept and face up to the anxiety of non-being.[11] The encounter with freedom in the deepest sense, therefore, is inseparable from the experience of courage.

If human freedom has any realistic meaning at all, it cannot mean deliverance *from* existential anxiety. The quest for freedom is destined for frustration as long as it is undertaken as the search for refuge from non-being. This is one lesson that theists can well learn from existentialist philosophers. In what then does human freedom consist (freedom in our second sense), if there is no easy escape from fate, death, guilt and the experience of doubt and even meaninglessness? Is human freedom even a meaningful notion, given the fact that our existence is never "free from" existential anxiety?

Humanly speaking, freedom is the awareness that existential anxiety has been *conquered* rather than simply evaded. It is an awareness that in spite of the pervasive threat of non-being, the core of our existence is always already ultimately secure. Such an awareness delivers us from the obsessive need to secure our existence in particular things and projects. It recognizes the futility of all such enterprises. And it allows for a serenity and peacefulness of existence that transcends the security which comes from our usual possessions.

But is such an awareness anywhere an actuality? Are there individuals who have achieved such a state of subjective freedom? I think that we do find such awareness exemplified in the lives of people who exhibit courage. It is not necessary to give examples of such courage here since we see it manifest all around us in the heroic lives of ordinary people who have themselves been motivated to courageous acceptance of their lives by their participation in the great stories of human courage passed down from generation to generation in all cultures and traditions. We have all witnessed the way in which people overcome apparently insurmountable difficulties and emerge as stronger in the process of facing their problems than if they had taken flight from them. This everyday occurrence is, in fact, so commonplace that we hardly notice its utterly "miraculous" character. It is in the lives of such courageous people that we can catch a glimpse of the ultimate horizon of freedom that seeks to liberate our human existence in a decisive way.

Human courage faces and accepts existential anxiety instead of fleeing from it. And in the act of facing it head-on it gives witness to a transcendent power capable of conquering the threat of non-being and providing a solid base for a realistic sense of freedom. We need not construct "proofs" for the "existence" of this power. The evidence for its reality is simply the acts of courage so manifest in the lives of those who accept themselves in spite of the existential anxiety that is part of their concrete existence.[12] In their courageous self-affirmation we can see evidence of their participation in an objective liberating "power" that conquers non-being. In viewing their heroic lives we can also appreciate the true meaning of human freedom as participating in an ultimate horizon of freedom—call it freedom-itself—which gives them the courage to prevail over the threats of non-being. Transparent in such lives of courage is a deep, transcendent freedom which has encircled their lives. Their courage is the "revelation" of an ultimate and abiding freedom that transcends and empowers our existence.

Our finite freedom (freedom in the second sense) is not a negative "freedom from" but rather a *participatory* freedom, an experience of opening oneself to and being grasped by the encompassing freedom that embraces and conquers the threat of non-being. This horizon of freedom of which we partake cannot be comprehended intellectually. It is not a possession, and it cannot be controlled by acts of "willfulness" on our part. It can only be experienced by oneself or pointed to as it becomes evident in the courageous lives of human persons. Its reality is felt only in the act of allowing oneself to be grasped by it. For that reason any scientific demonstration of its presence is impossible.

In the concrete lives of heroic people, moreover, we may also encounter the *fascinans,* fulfilling side of freedom. We may get an inkling of the dimension of freedom that corresponds with the "grounding" aspect of our experience of depth. And we also observe the foundation of what we called hope in the previous chapter.

The name of this ultimately grounding and courage-bestowing horizon of freedom that becomes transparent in acts of courage is—God. That grounding freedom is what the word "God" means. And if that word has not much meaning for you, translate it and speak of the deep freedom for which you yearn beyond the finite securities you cling to in order to escape existential anxiety. Perhaps in order to do this you must forget many things you have learned about "God," perhaps even that word itself. But as long as you open yourself to a courage whereby you realistically accept your existence, you cannot then call yourself an atheist in any meaningful sense of the term. For you cannot consistently maintain that there is no basis in reality for your courage. Even in your uttering such a statement you would give evidence of your participating in such a power of self-affirmation.

The Absence of God

A predictable response to our positing this ultimate, transcendent, liberating source of courage and referring to it as God is that such a suggestion seems superfluous. For we can readily identify specific persons, institutions such as family, school or country, nature itself or simply our biological vitality as the basis of our courage to face existential anxiety. It is our participation in these identifiable actualities that provides the sufficient foundation of our courage. Why should we needlessly complicate our picture of things by making reference to an "ultimate" power of being or horizon of freedom that lies hidden beyond the immediate or proximate sources of our courage?

Our response to this objection may begin with an appeal to human experience itself. A careful presentation of the facts of our individual and social histories renders plausible, though certainly not scientifically verifiable, our positing the reality of an ultimate source of courage not reducible to the proximate power sources referred to in the previous paragraph.

Let us reflect briefly on the typical ways we deal with our existential anxiety. I think honesty invites us to acknowledge that most of these ways turn out eventually to be failures, and that they do not deliver the freedom from anxiety that they initially promise. How, for example, do we confront the threats of fate and death? Of guilt and self-rejection? Of doubt and meaninglessness? Is it not usually by seeking the approval and acceptance of significant others in our *immediate* environment? The search for approval and acceptance seems to be an essential aspect of our being. And so it is understandable that we would begin very early in our lives, at the earliest inklings of our fragility, to win acceptance by pleasing those "powers," especially our parents, that seemingly have the strength to protect us from non-being. Such a maneuver does apparently work for a while, sometimes for years; and it is quite possible that we never succeed completely in detaching our existence from its earliest, seemingly omnipotent, parental power base. And if as adults it seems that we have finally outgrown a dependent relationship to our parents, we still have to ask to what degree we may have transferred our desire for parental approval onto others in our adult surroundings. To what extent do we stave off the threat of non-being by burying our existence in other proximate powers and authorities whose approval we so ardently desire?

As Ernest Becker has ingeniously shown, these proximate power sources to which we transfer our desire for deliverance from existential anxiety are eventually exposed as themselves subject to the same threats as we ourselves are. Becker develops this point in terms of the psychoanalytic notion of "transference." It may be instructive for us to follow some of his insights into the dynamics of this so-called transference.[13]

In psychoanalysis transference is understood as the displacement onto the analyst of both positive and negative feelings originally aroused by relationships to parents, siblings and significant others in our psychic history.[14] This distortive projection in the analytic encounter derives from the patient's compulsion to repeat inappropriately those patterns of affectivity that were learned in the earliest social relationships. But transference is not limited to the encounter of patient with analyst. It is a fact of everyday life as well. In our relationships with others we tend to transfer onto them unrealistic expectations (often going back to infancy and childhood) that have been frustrated time and again in the past. Transference in psychoanalysis is simply a heightened version of a commonplace occurrence.

According to Freud the dynamics underlying transference are fundamentally libidinal, even (and perhaps especially) when transference produces our gods. For others the energy behind transference is located in sources such as cowardice, the desire to escape freedom or the search for a power-source that will protect us from "reality" and, above all, from accepting our mortality. In whatever way it is understood, however, according to Becker the problem of transference is fundamentally a problem of courage.[15]

Becker envisions transference as a compromise between fear and courage. It is both a failure of courage and a search for it at the same time. As a manifestation of fear of life and death transference seeks to embed our lives in persons, institutions or other objects that seemingly engulf us and keep us from needing to stick out as individuals adventuring truly to live our lives on our own. Transference, according to this interpretation, is the habitual search for someone or something that will protect us from death and its individuating potential. By merging with omnipotent "others" through transference, we deliver ourselves of any necessity to face the chaos of death on our own. Thus transference seems to be a *flight* from the courage to accept both the freedom to live and the necessity of death.[16]

But is there no more to transference than a failure of courage? Is not transference a necessity of life? Becker interprets transference positively, and not just negatively, as the "urge to higher heroism." Transference is " . . . a form of creative fetishism, the establishment of a locus from which our lives can draw the powers they need and want."[17] In Paul Tillich's terms, then, we might interpret transference as not just a flight from courage but also a *quest* for power sources that mediate to us the courage to be. There is no unmediated participation in being. We participate in the ultimate power of being by way of beings. And if at times we endow specific finite beings with the transcendent qualities of being-itself, that is, of the divine, then this idolatry is understandable as an expression both of courage and its partial failure. Through transference we tend to focus the power of being which would be the adequate source of courage and freedom onto a narrow, restricted base. We want the transference object to function as itself omnipotent, and when it is apprehended as flawed by finitude it evokes in us the reaction of disillusionment and hostility. The gods of religions as well as certain images of God in theism partake of this ambiguity.

What makes transference unsatisfying, and therefore requires its transcendence, is that the provisional objects of transference cannot bear the full burden of being the ultimate, absolute, omnipotent sources of power and freedom we would like them to be. They happen to be finite, threatened by non-being themselves, and so they are unable to conquer the existential threat of non-being. Finite beings are symbolic of being; they participate in it and point to it, but they do not coincide with it. Thus they cannot accommodate the infinity of desire for ultimate security that energizes transference.

I think that the technique of frustration in psychoanalysis is an implicit recognition of this reality. The psychoanalyst must somehow resist the patient's attempts to squeeze out of the analytic encounter all the gratification that previous transference objects failed to deliver. And so the analyst cannot give in to the patient's demands that the former function as a God-figure for the latter. Nonetheless, the overcoming of transference cannot be accomplished by suppression of the patient's craving for a satisfying power source. The analyst, who is a heightened version of a whole series of disappointing power sources, cannot simply disavow the intense, perhaps infinite, quality of the patient's desires and demands. By refusal to play the role of the gratifying, omnipotent transference-object desired by the patient, the psychoanalyst implicitly acknowledges his or her own finitude and presents himself or herself to the patient as such. The analyst's technique of frustration is an implicit renunciation of any projected qualities of deity and an admission of the inability of one human being to function as an adequate savior figure for the other. But the nonjudgmental attitude of the analyst, the refusal to suppress the patient's desire, is implicitly a permission for the patient to seek out a broader, hopefully adequate, base for the transference-desire. Becker thinks that it is our quest for this adequate source of courage that energizes religious life and renders theistic religion intelligible as an appropriate context for "resolving" our transference tendencies.[18]

Therefore, the problem is not that we indulge in transference. This is a human inevitability, given the constant threat of non-being and our need to find some security in spite of it. Rather, the problem is that we usually direct our transference toward the nearest *finite* "beyond" instead of toward an infinite, transcendent beyond. As Becker says: ". . . people need a 'beyond,' but they reach first for the nearest one; this gives them the fulfillment they need but at the same time limits and enslaves them. . . . Most people play it safe: they choose the beyond of standard transfer-

ence objects like parents, the boss, or the leader. . . ."[19]
Because these transference objects are always limited in
their power to deliver us they cannot fulfill our longings for
an adequate power source or a foundational freedom.

However, the way out of our idolatrous projection of
impossible demands onto transference-objects is not simply
to renounce the transference altogether, as Freud at times
seemed to demand of the patient, but rather to allow the
transference to discover unimpeded the proportionate
objective of its intentionality, namely, an ultimate, transcendent power source. It goes without saying, of course,
that Freud would never have tolerated such an unscientific
manner of "resolving" the transference. And yet in an
oblique way even the founder of psychoanalysis hinted at
such a possibility. In a letter to the Protestant pastor, Oscar
Pfister, he seemed to acknowledge the religious dimension
of transference as well as the analyst's inability to respond
adequately to its demands:

> If the sick man had asked: "How knowest thou that my
> sins are forgiven?" the answer could only have been:
> "I, the Son of God, forgive thee." In other words, a call
> for *unlimited transference.* And now, just suppose I said
> to a patient: "I, Professor Sigmund Freud, forgive thee
> thy sins." What a fool I should make of myself.[20]

Often the first discovery of weakness in our "transference objects" is a moment of severe crisis for us. We find it
very difficult to admit and accept the finitude of spouse,
parents, or benign authorities we have trusted. We close our
eyes to the fragility of family life, the flaws of our country,
the utter fallibility of churches and other protective social
institutions. For without being reflectively aware of it we
have drawn from these realities the courage to accept our

lives in the face of non-being. These persons and institutions have mediated to us the vital energy we live by. To admit their own vulnerability is at times tantamount to drying up our power sources and to leaving us feeling utterly helpless. It is understandable, therefore, that we would project onto them an illusory omnipotence, an unrealistic numinosity that we hope will be proportionate to the anxiety of non-being we intuit as a constant accompaniment to our existence. We refuse to admit that we are thereby striving to turn these finite power sources into infinite ones. And the impossibility of this project is one that we usually do not acknowledge until we have experienced utter disillusionment.

When we have eventually experienced this disillusionment, we typically attempt to refashion our existence by turning to other near-at-hand, finite transference objects in our immediate environment. Often it is only after repeated attempts and utter frustration at finding a new and permanent power base that we turn explicitly to the quest for an ultimate source of courage, one that is proportionate to the depth of non-being over which our existence is situated. Often, though not necessarily, it is the experience of deep resentment at the finitude of our proximate power sources that leads us to acknowledge our desire for an infinite one, one that is not available to us within the realm of finite objects, persons and social arrangements. Experience of the inadequacy of our finite power sources may lead us to acknowledge the aptness of the religious idea of an "unavailable" ultimate power source in which our proximate power sources are themselves grounded.

The "absence of God," therefore, becomes intelligible to those who realize that no "visible" finite entity can all by itself be an adequate power base for the courage we need to accept our threatened existence. The demand that God be "visible" stems from a transference idolatry. Such a demand is implicitly a diminishment of our existence by chaining it exclusively to the fragility of finite, available, manipulable beings. The divine must be "absent" in order to transcend the finite status of our limiting transference objects. God must be "absent" in order to be the ground of our freedom.

Religion

Religion may be understood, in a normative way, as both the quest for and the affirmation of an ultimate ground of freedom—freedom not from but *in spite of* anxiety. Religion is constituted by a "symbolic sense" according to which finite realities are accepted as such and are not themselves burdened with the task of delivering us from existential anxiety. Religion is the conscious participation in an ultimate source of courage. This implies that religion relates to finite things in a special way. This way consists of enjoying them without absolutizing them. It is alert to the possibility of *idolatry*, of our imposing upon finite things the illusory expectation that they can by themselves give us the freedom we desire. It "sees through" them to the "power of being" by which they have their existence.

The ultimate power of being, however, cannot be experienced by us apart from its being embodied in finite realities. A naked and direct apprehension of the ultimate horizon of freedom and ground of courage is impossible. We intuit it, if at all, only as it becomes transparent by way of finite media. If we perceive its grounding reality showing through such things in a special or decisive way, then we may call these mediating events, persons or objects revelatory "symbols." If we experience these phenomena as symbolic it is only because we simultaneously perceive them as transparent to something infinitely more expansive than themselves. Thus ideally we do not confuse these finite realities with what they stand for. Essential to a genuine religious sense is an awareness that all objects and persons of our immediate environment participate in an ultimate "power of being," and by virtue of this participation are "revelatory" of some aspect of ultimate reality, but are not coextensive with that reality. Symbolic consciousness does not confuse the symbols with the symbolized. It does not try to squeeze ultimacy out of the objects of our immediate experience. It frees these objects to be simply themselves, namely symbols, and it does not impose unrealistic expectations upon them. For it sees them as revelatory of something greater in which they participate and from which they draw their own power to encourage and delight us. It takes great strength and courage to relate to finite entities in this manner. But it is only in such a relationship to them that true freedom can take hold of us.

It should be emphasized again that a properly symbolic sense allows us to enjoy and appreciate our immediate environment. It does not require a repudiation of the finite world, as do some distorted forms of religiosity. A symbolic sense does not call for an abandonment of or withdrawal from our "secular" surroundings. For inasmuch as it sees all things as participating in an ultimate power of being it pronounces them good. Each thing is capable of mediating ultimate reality in a unique and irreplaceable way. Each existent deserves our respect for its intrinsic worth. Furthermore, symbolic consciousness refuses to despair of our world and its history. Instead it looks into the world and history for new and deeper manifestations of its ultimate horizon. This attitude requires an immersion in our world and its history, not a gnostic escape from it.

At the same time a religious sense does demand that

we not clothe finite things in the guise of ultimate importance. And by freeing us from unrealistic attachment to immediate realities, religious symbolizing provides us with an anticipation of the freedom that is our deepest desire. It does so by its insistence that the symbols we relate to are not coextensively identical with that in which they participate and to which they point in their fragmentary way. A sense of this difference between symbol and symbolized, between beings and being, is often disturbing, and it constitutes one of the major stumbling blocks to the development of a courageous and liberating religious consciousness. The goodness and power of finite realities can appear so intoxicating at times that we fail to distinguish them from the ground in which they participate and which is the ultimate source of their own potency. We can become so entranced by them that they are no longer transparent to the infinite horizon of being. Our idolatrous attitude toward them wrenches them out of their proper metaphysical context and enshrines them in isolated splendor, insisting that, all by themselves, they bestow on us an ultimate deliverance. Their eventual failure to free us, however, is our opportunity for relocating them within the realm of symbols where once again they may be appreciated for what they really are.

To religious consciousness, then, all things are intrinsically symbolic. Our viewing them as symbols frees both them and us from being frozen in an identity that is too restricted. Symbolic consciousness bestows a sense of freedom by relating all things and all persons to an ultimate and infinite horizon of being. Religion is the search for and the anticipation of this horizon as the foundation of our freedom.

Chapter 4
Beauty

We have seen that the encounter with depth, futurity and freedom requires an attitude of allowing ourselves to be grasped by them. Our typical response, though, is one of initially shrinking back from entering into the embrace of these horizons (which are really three ways of thinking about a single horizon) while at the same time being irresistibly drawn toward them. Rather than allowing ourselves to be immediately comprehended by depth, futurity and freedom we try to place them under our control. Such a response is inevitably unsuccessful, however, and finally we realize that our sense of well-being, our happiness, requires that we surrender ourselves to them.

Nowhere is this need to surrender more obvious than in our encounter with beauty. In order for us to experience the beauty of nature, other persons, a great event or an artistic masterpiece, we have to allow ourselves to be "carried away" by the aesthetic phenomenon. This experience of being grasped by the beautiful is one of the clearest models we have for expressing what is involved in the intuition of the divine. In fact, it is more than a model. We may even say that our ordinary experience of the beautiful is already an encounter with ultimacy.

The experience of beauty is as two-sided as is the religious experience of the sacred. On the one hand, great beauty is overwhelming in its seductiveness and attractiveness. It is a *mysterium fascinans* that compels us and invites us to surrender ourselves to it. At times we have all experienced the seductiveness of the beautiful, especially as it is embodied in other persons, but also in the glories of nature, music and literature. At the same time we have felt the pangs of unfulfilled longing that accompany every aesthetic experience. We are implicitly aware of the chasm that lies between the beauty embodied in any particular object of aesthetic delight and the unlimited beauty for which we long in the depths of our desire. This abysmal distance is a *mysterium tremendum* from which we shrink back. Our recoil from ultimate beauty takes the form of a fixation on particular, limited aesthetic objects, and this fixation is accompanied by an anaesthetizing of our deep need for a wider and fuller beauty.

In short, our quest for beauty is a quest for the divine. That ultimately satisfying beauty for which we long but which continues to elude us is what the word "God" means. And if that word has not much meaning for you, translate it and speak of the ultimately beautiful for which you are continually searching in the depths of your desire. Perhaps in order to do this you must forget much that you have learned about God, perhaps even that name itself. For if you know that God means ultimate "beauty," you already know much about the divine. You cannot then call yourself an atheist, for you cannot think or say, "I am completely indifferent to beauty." If you could say this in complete seriousness then you would be an atheist. But otherwise you are not. For as long as you have some longing for a wider and deeper beauty than you have experienced thus far in your life you show that you have already in some way encountered the divine, or rather that the divine has taken hold of you. Another way to think about God, therefore, is as the horizon of ultimate beauty toward which you are irresistibly drawn.

Scholars of religion often make a distinction between religious and aesthetic experience (as we shall call the experience of beauty). Religion, they often say, involves the symbolic sense of a "totally other" dimension that becomes transparent to the believer in the images and objects that stand for and mediate the "sacred." The aesthetic experience, on the other hand, is not explicitly concerned with the symbolic transparency of the aesthetic object. It does not have to understand a beautiful object as standing for any sacred reality "beyond" itself. The beautiful seems sufficient in itself and does not inevitably lead us into another dimension, whereas the religious sense does.[1] To many individuals for whom the "sacred" means nothing at all the "beautiful" means a great deal. Therefore, some distinction must be made between "the sacred" and "the beautiful."

But can we so neatly set one experience apart from the other? I am uncomfortable with too sharp a distinction between aesthetic and religious experience. To segregate them too crisply seems artificial and out of touch with what actually happens in our encounter with the beauty of reality. For if we carefully ponder what is involved in the experience of concrete beauty, we may think of it as continuous with our encountering the divine. By our tasting the beauty in our ordinary experience we are already being invited into the realm of ultimacy, though we may not wish to interpret it as such. Nonetheless, the point of the following is to argue that this is indeed the case. An examination of our ordinary encounter with beauty may disclose to us that the beautiful too is a *mysterium tremendum et fascinans,* and that we respond to it with the same ambivalent wavering between repulsion and attraction that the experience of the sacred evokes in *homo religiosus.*

Can we state conceptually what it is that makes things appear to us as beautiful and some things as more beautiful than others? Alfred North Whitehead, whose philosophy is permeated by aesthetic considerations, tells us that beauty is the "harmony of contrasts." What makes us appreciate the beauty of things is that they bring together nuance, richness, complexity and novelty on the one side, and harmony, pattern or order on the other. The more "intense" the synthesis of harmony and contrast, the more we appreciate their union. Nuance without harmony is chaos, and harmony without nuance is monotony. Beauty involves the transformation of potentially clashing elements into pleasing contrasts harmonized by the overarching aesthetic pattern of the beautiful object or experience.[2]

An example of such harmony of contrasts may be seen in any great novel. What makes such a novel beautiful is its weaving together into a unified whole the many subplots and characterizations that might easily have led to confusion. A poor novel would be one that was so concerned with overall order that it failed to establish sufficient tension and conflict to bring about the nuanced complexity required by beauty. At the opposite extreme, an inferior novel would degenerate into chaos by failing to bring its details into the unity of a single story. Either lack of harmony or absence of complexity would impoverish the artistic masterpiece. Our appreciation of the work of art, or of anything beautiful, is the result of our implicit sense that the beautiful precariously balances the order and novelty brought together in the aesthetic object.

If we reflect on the elements of the beautiful, however,

we are led to the conclusion, also emphasized by White-head, that *every* actuality is, to some degree at least, an aesthetic phenomenon. Every "actual entity" is a patterned synthesis of contrasting elements. In the simplest objects the contrasts are not intense, but they are there at least to some small degree. Nothing would be actual at all unless its ingredients were patterned in some way or other. Whether we are talking about an electron, an artistic creation, a person, a civilization or the universe as such, these entities would not have any identity whatsoever unless their constituent elements were patterned in a definite way. Their "actuality" corresponds by degrees to the mode and intensity of their synthesizing harmony and contrast. This means that all things are actual to the extent that they are beautiful, and all things are beautiful to the extent that they order novelty and complexity into aesthetic contrasts.[3]

Beauty, therefore, has what philosophers call a "transcendental" nature. This means that "the beautiful" is not any particular thing, but instead is a metaphysical aspect of all things. (Being, truth, unity, goodness and beauty are the "transcendentals" usually mentioned by metaphysicians.) For this reason alone we may suspect that we cannot casually disassociate any possible encounter with beauty from the experience of the divine, which is said to be the supreme exemplification of the "transcendentals."

We experience beauty in nature, in the physical appearances or personalities of others, in great architecture, art, music, poetry and other types of literature. But one of the most intense instances of aesthetic experience lies in the spectacle of an heroic story. Since such stories involve the *narrative patterning* of struggle, suffering, conflicts and contradictions into a complex unity, they stand out as one of the most obvious examples of beauty. In fact, it is often our being conditioned by the stories of great heroes that determines our whole sense of reality, personal identity and purpose, as well as the quality of our aesthetic experience in general. From the beginning of human history it appears that the consciousness of people, their sense of reality, identity and destiny, has been shaped primarily by their sense of the heroic as it is deposited in the paradigmatic *stories* of their traditions. In myth, legend, ballad, history, epic and other types of story people have woven around themselves a narrative womb with all the ingredients of ordered contrast that I am here attributing to beauty.

The identity of all of us is established by our interaction with the narrative context of our existence. Our sense of the meaning of our lives, if we are fortunate enough to be conscious of living meaningfully, is a gift of the narrative nest in which we dwell. The meaning of our lives is determined by the way in which each of us participates in an ongoing story. And where people today speak of their experience of meaninglessness, isolation, alienation, rootlessness etc., such experiences can almost invariably be traced to an inability to find some meaningful story in which to situate their lives.[4]

Belonging to a story wherein the contradictions and conflicts in one's own life-experience are patterned into a larger harmony by the narrative's harmonizing of contrast is one of the most intimate experiences we can have of the beautiful. Such a narrative encounter with beauty, I repeat, is what makes a meaningful life possible for us in the first place. It is by allowing ourselves to be taken up into some power-bestowing narrative which patterns the moments of our lives that we are given the courage to accept the existential threats discussed in the preceding chapter. The sense of a wider beauty that situates our own experiences within an aesthetically intense pattern is indispensable to the feeling of living in hopeful freedom. And it is the function of the narrative context of our lives to provide this patterning.

When there is no deep impression that the apparent contradictions in our lives are being resolved into aesthetic contrasts by the unfolding of a comprehensive narrative in which our struggles, sufferings and joys are embedded, there is the experience of meaninglessness. The feeling that one does not belong to anything greater than oneself, the pain of isolation from any heroic struggle that would give continuity to the chaotic moments of one's life, is at bottom the lack of a sense of participating in the beautiful.

There is, however, an interesting paradox involved in the lives of those who are no longer attuned to the stories that give meaning to the lives of their fellows. Often those most alienated from the aesthetic harmony provided by traditional narratives of human origin, identity and destiny are the most creative artists in any given period. How are we to make sense of this paradox? It is almost as though the really creative geniuses had to be jolted out of the warmth and security of the narrative nest occupied by their contemporaries and made to fly away in disorientation and agonizing isolation at least for a period. And to some degree at least, maybe a temporary disorientation is essential for the aesthetic intensification of the experience of all of us. Though some who have taken flight have lost their bearings and succumbed to madness, suicide or quiet despair, others have become creators and brought novelty and depth to the human search for beauty. Creativity is accompanied by the threat of disorder, and this seems to be the inevitable risk of intense aesthetic achievement. But does the creative genius of unique individuals who have become disillusioned with our stories not contradict the thesis that we need a narrative context to give aesthetic patterning to our lives?

It is said that we now live in an age in which narrative is losing its hold on consciousness, if not in the everyday life of the average person, at least in that of the critically

minded and creative individual. Even a few scholars of religion are now suggesting that the age of story is undergoing
a "closure."[5] It would be hard to gather sociological data to
support this proposition, especially given the pervasive participation by people the world over in political and religious
ideologies whose very power consists of their weaving
human lives into specific types of "heroic" stories. However, whatever we may think about the sociology of these
scholars, they make a valid point when they trace the
decline of a narrative sense to the modern disillusionment
with the idea of transcendence. The "death of God" does
seem to entail the collapse of narrative as the matrix for our
lives. The inability to think about God in any meaningful
sense undermines the idea of there being any overarching
meaning to history or to the universe as such. And when
the cosmos and history are themselves perceived as pur-
poseless, then the individual's life-story (if one can call it a
story at all) will be seen as nothing more than a disjointed
series of moments played out on a stage that is deaf to any
cry for meaning. Without the support of a transcendent
ground, therefore, life-inspiring narrative can be no more
than a chimera. Once people begin to suspect that there is
no such ground, the cosmic and historic narratives that
attempt to locate their lives in the total scheme of things
will also lose their power. One must, therefore, applaud
those authors who have been consistent enough in their
thinking to connect the demise of story to a sense of the
death of God, and vice versa.[6]

A clear example of the attempt to draw this logical
inference and to situate human experience outside of any
meaning-bestowing story may be observed in Albert
Camus' novel *The Stranger*. The stranger, Meursault, is an
outsider to all social conventions and traditions. He does
not weep at his mother's funeral, fails to get involved in the

"normal" project of making a name for himself or of carving out a career, feels indifferent toward marriage, senselessly kills an Arab, refuses to cooperate in his own defense and serenely awaits his execution. Throughout his life he has no hope for the future and feels no guilt or regret about his past. He lives only in the present, though not necessarily hedonistically. He feels he is a part of nature with its sun, sex and seashores, but he is not a part of any history that might link his present to a significant past or a promising future. His life is a series of disjointed, unpatterned monads of experience with no story-line tying them together. He rejects as dishonest any attempt on the part of society or its religious representatives to fit his life into some universal narrative scheme. In particular the idea of an afterlife, where the human story would presumably be "wrapped up," is repulsive to him.

And yet Meursault is "happy." As he awaits the guillotine he experiences a sense of "freedom" denied to those imprisoned by stories of cosmic and historical meaning. He is an outsider to narrative because he senses the mutual implication of God, justice and story. If there is no justice, then there is no God, and if there is no God, then there is no basis for meaning-bestowing stories. The fact of death is sufficient to show that there is no ultimate fairness or justice, and so the repudiation of God and story follows from that simple fact. Religion and society, though, are held together by story, a story that has to be built dishonestly on the denial of death. A simple sense of honesty about death, on the other hand, should lead by way of simple logic to a conviction of the indifference of the universe. And the same lucidity should convince us of the deceitful character of all narratively based ideologies that coat over the world's fundamental unintelligibility with seductive stories of ultimate meaning.

We can see in Camus' brilliant novel an illustration of
the simultaneous loss of a sense of God, self-identity, history and story. Without the backing of a meaningful cosmic
story grounded in the care of a transcendent divine reality
the individual's experience in modern times has often been
felt as itself devoid of any meaningful pattern. If the cosmic
context is cold and indifferent to the individual's life experience, then the truly creative individual has no choice but
to set out to forge completely new beauty. Thus the absence
of God, myth, tradition and history, painfully isolating as it
is, is perceived by some modern writers in this allegedly
storyless world as an unprecedented aesthetic opportunity.
The void left by the death of God may be filled with the
products of our own creativity. For, as Nietzsche put it,
"what could man create if gods existed?"

Any attempt on our part to think of God today cannot
ignore, but must instead appropriate, this modern disillusionment with the kind of aesthetic experience found in
story. It must respect the sincerity of those who have seemingly broken with our traditional stories. For it is entirely
possible that the same stories that give some of us meaning
are too narrow, in their typical versions, to accommodate
the idiosyncratic experience and suffering of some very creative individuals. The experience of these tormented artists
may be the occasion for our widening our stories in order
that the latter might take into account even the modern
experience of storylessness.

I would suggest, then, that the apparent breakdown of
a narrative sense is not necessarily a signal of the absolute
vanishing of a sense of transcendence. Rather it may be
understood as an essential moment of dismantling restrictive narrative structures, a clearing operation that paves the
way for a wider and "more beautiful" notion of the depth
of reality. The experience of the "end of story" is, in short,

an experience of the *mysterium tremendum,* of the abyss that yawns between our particular aesthetic obsessions and the wider narrative of an ultimate beauty that alone can satisfy. In our hunger for an ultimately satisfying aesthetic experience, a hunger testified to in a pre-eminent way by the storyless artists of our age, any local cosmic, mythic, nationalistic, historic or religious patterning of experience will be perceived as too narrow, as the substitution of a sketch for the whole picture.[7] And so the quest for the truly beautiful involves what might be called a "deconstruction" of narrative contexts that are too narrow to situate aesthetically all the complexity and chaos of contemporary experience.

"Deconstructionism" is the name given to a significant, particularly French, strain of contemporary philosophy and literary criticism. It pulls together a number of elements of suspicion, criticism and even nihilism that can be found in modern thought, and so it is a useful exemplification of the disillusionment with story that I am discussing here. Its name refers to the program of deconstructing or dismantling any type of thinking or language that is conditioned by the traditional sense that there is a transcendent reality standing behind and signified by ordinary events and language. And since virtually all of our traditional language and literature has been molded in the crucible of theistically influenced assumptions about a "transcendental signified," nothing less than a complete dismantling of traditional discourse is required by deconstructionism.[8]

Traditionally belief in God led us to believe that history is providentially patterned in a narrative way involving the movement of events from the creation, through the present period of historical struggle, and climaxing at the end of time with the complete arrival of the "kingdom of God." This narrative structure with its "sense of an ending" has in turn shaped the consciousness of writers and thinkers (as well as ordinary individuals) so that a narrative way of patterning life experience has become almost universal in Western culture. The Bible and even the very notion of "book" as such are based on the assumption that reality has a narrative structure to it. And the individual living in the context of a culture shaped by the "Book" is given his or her sense of personal identity by the hierarchy of stories ultimately rooted in the story of God.[9]

Deconstructionists are extremely sensitive to the role of narrative in patterning the consciousness of the West, even in its secular forms (such as Marxism and humanism). However, they are also alert to the fact that the whole narrative edifice, consisting of the universal story of salvation and all the minor stories dramatized beneath this narrative umbrella, is ultimately rooted in the sense of the transcendent. What, then, would be the implications of the "death of God," of the absence of any universal ground of meaning? Nothing less than a complete collapse of the entire narrative hierarchy. If the horizon of the transcendent is wiped away, as it has been in some post-Enlightenment consciousness, then all the stories inscribed on our consciousness according to the beginning-struggle-fulfillment model of Western religion have no validity whatsoever. No longer can we entrust ourselves to the aesthetic patterning of our inherited heroic stories or allow them to give us a sense of identity and meaning. Indeed it is questionable whether identity and meaning are now possible at all. It is highly doubtful whether language and writing can refer to anything beyond themselves. Human discourse and literature are nothing more than the "play" of words without any transcendent signification. The death of a sense of the sacred means literally the death of story, the end of history, the demise of the "Book" and the collapse of self-identity into absolute anonymity.[10] Camus' "stranger" has now become the anonymously ideal everyman.

In our attempts to think of God it would be too easy for us simply to dismiss this deconstructionist enterprise as just another type of nihilism parasitically feeding on worn-out ideas of Nietzsche and French existentialism. For in any aesthetic understanding of ultimate reality, such as the one I am presenting here, "deconstructionist" moments are necessary to add nuance and intensity to the aesthetic whole. Without such nuance there will be an intolerable monotony, just as without harmony there will be complete chaos. Sometimes an outrageous demand for chaos is a way of expressing revulsion with a stifling monotony. But disgust with monotony is simply the other side of our deep need for beauty. Buried in the blessed rage for chaos is a hidden longing for ultimate beauty. In their protest against the confinement of narrative, "deconstructionists" of all ages evince a longing for absolute beauty with which we can identify the depth of religious desire as well.

In this light the "deconstructionist" element in modern criticism, in its seemingly nihilistic dismantling of tradition, history, religion and story, may be interpreted as itself a moment of contrast that adds nuance to the wider pattern of beauty for which we remain forever nostalgic. The way in which human consciousness has at times been frozen in particular narrative patterns deserves the kind of negative criticism one finds in a deconstructionist philosophy. In spite of its inevitable protests to the contrary I would suggest that, like Nietzsche, its criticism is directed less at narrative as such than at *narrative fixation.* Deconstructionists are by no means the most significant threat to the integrity of story. For the demise of story is first of all the result of our childish obsession with particular versions of a dynamic narrative tradition. The attempt to freeze a particular tradition in an absolutely conservative way is already the end of story, the true "nihilism" that prevents the story from remaining alive. Story-fixations bring about the end of story, and with it the impression of the death of God, long before modern deconstructionists begin their work. Nietzsche himself was well aware of the implicit nihilism buried in the superficial narrative fixation of much Christian theology and spirituality. By bringing the "ending" into narrative view prematurely, by failing to *wait* in the midst of struggle, and by narrowing the ending down to dimensions too suffocating to satisfy the human desire for the infinite, story-fixation is itself already the death of narrative. To be properly narrative the cosmic and human story must remain in process. To freeze the story artificially is to kill it. Hence the deconstruction of story(-fixation) of which we have been speaking is an essential nullifying operation undertaken for the sake of the survival of narrative itself. The stories, histories and cosmologies taken apart by deconstructionists are, in my view, highly caricatured versions with which some, but by no means all, believers are uncomfortable anyway. Although its proponents would undoubtedly deny it, deconstructionism announces not the end of story as such, but rather the end of naive story-fixations. And thus it may be seen as contributing in the final analysis to a wider aesthetic vision.

However, the narrative sense which our critics have rightly tied to the idea of God is incapable of being absolutely eradicated. Their own writings display a narrative undercurrent of which they are not always aware. They themselves tell a story about story. Their tale has a beginning, a period of struggle, and an end. Deconstructionists envisage themselves as living in the "final days," when history and narrative have come to an end, when an eternal "play" of language eschatologically appears.[11] Ironically they usually invoke and transform ancient myths (stories) like those of Sisyphus, Eros, Thoth, Prometheus, Zarathustra and others to instruct us about the futility of myth. In the very performance of the deconstruction of narrative they give evidence of the ineradicably narrative quality of all human experience and consciousness.

In its announcing the "closure" (which does not necessarily mean chronological end) of history, self and narrative, and in its endorsement of a formless and insignificant play of language, therefore, deconstructionism also falls short of giving us the ultimate aesthetic fulfillment we all long for. In the final analysis this philosophy is not a space within which one can live. If it has any value at all in terms of our aesthetic needs it is only as a "moment" in the process of moving toward a wider narrative vision of beauty than is allowed by our story-fixations. Unfortunately, in its repudiation of the tension intrinsic to narrative, and in its artificial efforts to force the eschaton of play into the temporal narrowness of the present, it is reduced to one more version of the gnostic escapes from history to which religious people are always tempted whenever they grow tired of waiting and struggle. Once again it is worth recalling Tillich's words: "We are stronger when we wait than when we possess." This applies not only to our search for depth but also to our quest for an ultimate beauty.

The Absence of God

The quest for a completely satisfying aesthetic experience always leaves us with some element of discontent. In the first place intense experience of beauty never lasts indefinitely. The most memorable sensations we have of being carried away by beauty are often only instants that quickly fade and that resist adequate repetition. In the second place there is always a region of our aesthetic longing that remains unfulfilled even by the most poignant encounters with beautiful persons, music, art or natural phenomena. It is not difficult for any of us to conjure up examples from our own lives of the elusiveness of beauty. Seemingly we are unable completely to control the beautiful but must instead patiently await the summons to be taken into its grasp.

The experience of never being completely filled up by particular aesthetic experiences is of course frustrating. It might even tempt one to an "absurdist" interpretation of reality. The inability of particular aesthetic manifestations to satisfy the infinity of our desire for the sublime might easily be construed as just another instance of the insuperable incongruity of man and universe. And it would be very difficult to offer an empirical refutation of this tragic view.

However, there is another at least equally plausible interpretation of our aesthetic frustration. It stems from our thesis that ultimately the beautiful is the divine, a *mysterium tremendum et fascinans.* And if the divine is the beautiful or sublime, then, in keeping with what we have noted in each of the preceding chapters, we should expect not so much to grasp beauty as to allow it to comprehend us and carry us away into itself. However, as we have also emphasized, our initial instinct is usually that of resisting and even denying the gentle envelopment of our existence by the *mysterium,* in this case, the beautiful. Aesthetic frustration, therefore, is not so much a failure on the part of the beautiful to meet us as it is the result of our shrivelling our aesthetic sensitivity to restrictive dimensions that "protect" us from the beautiful. The "absurdist" interpretation would insist that our aesthetic frustration is the result of the fact that while we ourselves have an insatiable, even infinite, capacity for experiencing beauty, reality is limited in its ability to satisfy our needs. Hence absurdism places the source of our frustration in the universe itself instead of in the possible limitedness of our own aesthetic perceptivity.

The view that I am presenting, on the other hand, holds that the "doors" of our perception are possibly too narrow to let in the fullness of the beautiful, while the inner chamber of our consciousness continues to ache in emptiness for a beauty that would fill it and to which our perceptivity is inadequate. Aesthetic frustration stems from the inadequacy of our perceptive faculties to the deep inner need we have for limitless beauty. The absurdist view seems to be based on an unrealistic notion of perception.

Whitehead has shown how an unduly narrow doctrine of perception has dominated most of modern thought, including our understanding of beauty.[12] According to the commonly accepted view of modern empirically oriented thought the five senses are the only doors of our perception. If we are to be in touch with the real world we are instructed to attend primarily to the data given to the mind by the senses of taste, touch, smell, sound and especially sight (aided of course by scientific instruments of perception). But without denying that our senses do put us in touch with the real world, Whitehead emphasizes that the senses give us only a very abstract and narrow range of the universe. They are inadequate to mediate the full complexity—and beauty— of the world in which we are organically situated. They bite off only a very narrow range of the contemporary world and leave behind the unfathomable temporal depths and aesthetic intensity of the universe as a whole. And so we typically tend to ignore the wider aesthetic patterning of reality since it is left out by the clear and crisp impressions given to us by the five senses.

However, we also have a deeper and more comprehensive mode of sensitivity that lies beneath the clarity of sense perception. In a total bodily or "visceral" mode of sensitivity we are constantly feeling aspects of reality that go beyond the clear data of sense perception. In our entire organism we are linked to the dynamic tides of an evolving universe in ways that are not clearly presented by our sense impressions. In a vague and cloudy way we are ourselves *being patterned by* an aesthetic whole, the universe, in ways that we are not explicitly aware of, and in a manner that we cannot control. Our being shaped by this larger totality is a "causal" mode of perception, deeper if not clearer than sense perception. In the very process of our being influenced by the universe in which we are embedded we are actually feeling or "perceiving" the cosmos at a more fundamental level than sense perception. Thus sense perception is only a thin external veneer of the deeply organic feeling we have of reality as it patterns our experiences and synthesizes our existence into itself.

By distinguishing between the sharply defined region of sense data and the vaguer but deeper organic perception that lies beneath sensation, Whitehead gives us a doctrine of perception that allows us to understand the "absence of God" as well. God is necessarily hidden from the realm of sense objects simply because sense perception is too narrow to give us the deeper and more important aspects of reality. Sense perception cannot even put us in touch with the wider aesthetic patterning of our universe. How, then, can we expect our senses, oriented as they are toward the present moment, to give us a clear representation of that which is said to be the source of the world's beauty and the ultimate destiny of its aesthetic evolution? The demand that God be available in the region of sensibly verifiable entities is rooted in an inadequate philosophy of perception. Ironically this philosophy, in spite of its lip service to the empirical imperative, is quite unempirical in its ignoring the deeper aspects of our perceptivity, and it is dogmatic in its restricting perception to the top level of our many-layered feeling of the universe.

If our ordinary perceptivity is inadequate to the wider aesthetic patterning even of our universe, then it would surely follow that it would also be inadequate to any "ultimate" beauty that transcends the universe itself. Therefore, a more expansive doctrine of perception, such as Whitehead's, should allow us to accept intellectually the unavailability of God to any verificational process seeking sensible clarity and distinctness. It is not that the divine is not experienced in any way at all. Rather, the point is that our *sense* perception is too restrictive to contain the fullness of beauty that is the divine. It would be more accurate to say that (by way of the "causal" mode of perception) we experience the fullness of beauty comprehending us than that we perceive this beauty as just another controllable datum of perception. This experience, though, is deeper and vaguer than sense experience and therefore is not as obvious in its clarity as we might wish. Hence it is easily ignored or repressed. But the absence of God from the narrow range of objects of sense perception is necessary if we are to experience (and be experienced by) the infinite beauty that is the divine.

The experience of aesthetic frustration at not being able to fill ourselves sufficiently with beauty can become tolerable if we allow ourselves and our lives to be taken up into a patterning by ultimate beauty rather than obsessively attempting to place it within our control. Frustration, as the Buddha taught, is the result of misplaced desire. And, as all the major traditions of religious and philosophical wisdom have agreed, the renunciation of desires incommensurate wtih the finite status of our existence is the indispensable condition of any properly human contentment. This is as much the case with regard to aesthetic longing as with any of our desires. *We must allow our own desire to grasp the beautiful to become transformed into a desire to be grasped by*

beauty itself. Concretely this would mean that we let ourselves and our life stories be taken up into the unfathomable evolutionary story of the universe itself. We would have
to forego any attempt to superimpose coercively the narrowness of our own stories onto this unimaginable whole.
We would have to accommodate ourselves to the fact that
we do not have any universal, absolute vantage point
whereby to appreciate the entire cosmic canvas as it
unfolds. We are after all only a small part of the ongoing
narrative of a universal aesthetic patterning, and so we are
not in a position to comprehend the complete picture. Our
lives, with their joys and sorrows, may contribute what
Whitehead calls "needed contrast" to the universal cosmic
story, but we may have no mastering grasp of it. Instead,
the universal story of beauty seeks to take us into itself and
invites us to make our lives a contribution to it. The meaning of our lives is to surrender to the creative synthesis of
this narratively aesthetic process, to make our own lives
part of a process of an ongoing deepening of the beauty of
the universe. And in order to make this self-donation we
must forfeit our impulse to render the divine a possession
verifiable in terms of the limitedness of presently available
sense data. We must accept the "absence of God" as a necessary condition for the aesthetic intensity and significance
of our own lives.

Religion

If the divine is thought of as ultimate beauty, then how
may we understand religion? Religion, in the widest sense,
may be thought of as the pursuit of the beautiful, as devo-
tion or surrender to the cosmic process that orders novelty
into more intense aesthetic contrasts and so enhances the
incarnation of beauty in our world. The name Whitehead

gives to the ongoing quest for more and more intense forms of ordered novelty is *adventure*.[13] And in its pure, undistorted essence this is what religion is. Religion is adventure.

The term "adventure" immediately suggests risk. Any adventurous proceeding necessarily involves an element of risk without which there would be nothing truly "ventured." What exactly is the risk involved in adventure? Again we may respond in terms of the elements of the aesthetic theory we have been following.[14] Since adventure always involves the search for novelty, there is a risk that the bringing of new aspects into any presently ordered situation will be accompanied by the threat of disorder since the old order has to give way and make room for the new. Almost inevitably there will be a moment of disorder or deconstruction as the elements are reconstructed into a more intense pattern. The introduction of novelty can be so disruptive at times that there is even the threat of chaos. We have already seen that in order to have beauty there must be a balance of harmony with contrast and of order with novelty. Without the contrast provided by novelty there will be an unaesthetic monotony. But without a harmonious ordering there will be the ugliness of discord. So the risk involved in any adventurous quest for novelty is an aesthetic risk, the risk of a disorder that overwhelms the harmony required to transform conflicts, clashes and contradictions into aesthetically satisfying contrasts. On the other hand, if there is a need for novel convolutions or nuance as, for example, in the writing of a novel, and the author resists twisting the plot, then the result will be an intolerably trivial production, one that fails to capture our aesthetic interest. In this case there is the risk of monotony, and this also means a failure to achieve beauty.

The universe that we inhabit may itself be understood—and science supports this position—as an adventure. It appears to be a fifteen or twenty billion-year-old quest for more and more intense forms of ordered novelty. As it has evolved from pre-atomic elements to the emergence of life, and then to the appearance of humanity and civilization, it seems to have experimented with endless varieties of ordered novelty. These adventurous experiments have evaded monotony only by risking the chaos of extinction by natural selection and other pressures of evolution. And our human history chronicles a similar story of adventures leading either to chaos or to creative advance. Whenever advance (measured aesthetically in terms of the intensity of ordered novelty) has taken place, it has always been at great risk to prevailing forms of order.

Religion must be seen as continuous with the universe's risk-filled episodes of adventure. Otherwise it is unrelated to the rest of reality. If it is a truly appropriate and significant evolutionary development, and not just another blind alley, then religion must embody the spirit of adventure. At its best it has always done so. But at its worst it has contributed much ugliness to civilization.[15] More often than not, perhaps, concrete historical religions have allied themselves with the forces of monotony. Because they teach a doctrine of ultimate order their teachings are easily perverted into divine sanctions for a *particular* (non-ultimate) empirical socio-political order. Religion then becomes little more than the sacral legitimation of the status quo. As such it functions to impede the advance of beauty. "Religion" then feeds on our distaste for adventure. And it loses its vitality whenever it forfeits the risk required by an openness to novelty. A purely conservative religion, while manifesting an understandable passion for order, promotes the stagnation of monotony and narrative fixation. And if we have appropriately identified the divine with the beautiful, then such religion is opposed to any full surrender to the ultimate.

At its normative best, however, religion has also been the most adventurous component in the historical evolution of human consciousness. Its openness to novelty and the risk involved in this openness are evidenced in the great religious innovators and visionaries (for example, the Buddha, Moses, the prophets, Jesus, Paul, Muhammad, Francis, Luther, etc., and their devotees). Theirs have been the most disturbing and discordant voices of all. But the chaos they have often left in their wake is not the result of any deliberately deconstructionist doctrine of disorder on their part. Rather it is the consequence of their vision of an ultimate, transcendent order that includes the widest possible novelty and contrast. In attempting to implant their vision into the contemporary scope of human awareness they and their disciples have inevitably disturbed the monotony of the status quo. A truly adventurous religious spirit will always disrupt the cult of monotony at the same time at which it promises ultimate contentment.

It seems to me that if we can distill any common element from the extreme diversity of adventurous religions it is the following exhortation: Do not settle for an order that is too narrow for you. By all means follow your passion for order, since without order there is nothingness. But strive for an order that is tolerant of novelty and conflicts. The ultimately satisfying order is not a harmony attained by suppressing conflict among the elements that make it up. Be open to novelty even if it produces a temporary discord, for in the larger scheme of things that lies beyond your present comprehension, beauty will prevail. Ultimate beauty will insure that all manner of things shall be well. The depth of your existence, your absolute future, the ground of your freedom, is ultimate beauty.

Chapter 5
Truth

What do we want more than anything else? What is our deepest desire? How many of us can honestly respond: "The truth—what we want most is the truth about the universe, about other people, and especially about ourselves"; Is truth what we really want most deeply? Or would we not be better off if we were spared the truth? Søren Kierkegaard wrote: " . . . it is far from being the case that men in general regard relationship with the truth as the highest good, and it is far from being the case that they, Socratically, regard being under a delusion as the greatest misfortune."[1] Why is it that we are not always interested in truth and instead often seek refuge in illusions?

Perhaps the reason is that the desire for truth is not the only passion governing our conscious and instinctive lives. Only a little reflection is needed to remind us that we are composed of a morass of drives, desires, longings, cravings, wishes and hopes. Curiously the inhabitants of this jungle of desires are often in conflict with one another. One part of us might want sensual gratification, another security, another power, another meaning, another approval. Furthermore, one desire may be superimposed upon another, so that their disentanglement seems nearly impossible. It is often hard to determine which of the desires is dominant or to which of our various inclinations we should entrust the course of our lives. Often we experiment with a variety of our urges before we commit ourselves to any one of them as our fundamental option. Perhaps a serious pursuit of truth is one of the last of our desires to be accepted as a dynamic force in our lives because there is so much competition from other urges that are quite content to live with illusions.

And yet the message of our great religious, literary and philosophical classics is that there is really only one desire that we can completely trust to lead us to genuine happiness, namely our thirst for the truth. Only when we subordinate our other inclinations to the *eros* for truth will we find what we are really looking for. And yet how dominant is this desire in our own conscious existence? Perhaps the passion to get to the truth has not yet assumed a central role in our lives. "I want the truth" may be only a tentative, barely audible utterance buried under many layers of longing that are not at all interested in the truth. We may at times wonder why the prophets, visionaries and philosophers have made so much of the pursuit of truth, especially if there is little inclination for it in our own lives.

What is the truth? Can it be defined? Or do we not implicitly appeal to it even in trying to define it, so that any attempted definition is circular? It would be an interesting experiment if you would pause at this point and attempt to define "truth." The classical definition of truth is the "correspondence of mind with reality." But what is reality? Can it be defined? The term truth not only often refers to the cognitional stance of one who is in touch with "reality," but it may also be used interchangeably with reality itself. That is, truth may be understood either epistemologically (as referring to the correspondence of our minds to reality) or metaphysically (as the name for that reality our minds are in touch with). In one sense truth means the attunement of the mind to being, to the real, to the true. In the following, however, I shall use the term "truth" primarily in the metaphysical sense, namely, as "being," the "real" or the "true" which is intended as the goal of our desire for reality. In other words I shall use the terms truth, being and reality interchangeably.

It seems that in the case of truth we are dealing once again with an "horizon" that evades our efforts at intellectual control and adequate definition. If anything, truth would define us more than we would define it. The encounter with truth is more a case of our being grasped by it than of our actively grasping it.

Perhaps, therefore, we can speak of the truth only in a "heuristic" sense, that is, as something we are seeking but which never allows itself to be completely ensnared by our instruments of discovery. We can speak of truth more as the "objective" or goal of a certain kind of wanting within us than as a possession firmly within our grasp. Yet even though we cannot possess the truth or get our minds around it, we can at least recognize clearly, among the multiplicity of our wants, a *desire* for the truth, even if it is not yet a powerful impulse. A brief reflection on your own thinking process will confirm the presence of this desire in your consciousness.

You may just now have asked: "Is it really the case that something in me wants the truth?" You need no further or more immediate evidence that you do have some such desire. The simple fact that you ask such a question is evidence enough.

It is in the asking of such questions, indeed of any

questions at all, that we have the most obvious evidence of our undeniable longing for the truth. We may call this longing simply the *desire to know*. It may not yet be highly developed within us. It may be only a whisper that is easily ignored, an occasional impulse readily repressed. And yet it may well be the deepest and most ineradicable part of ourselves, the very essence of our being. It may turn out that of all our longings and wild wishings our desire to know is the only one whose ardor we can give into with completely trusting abandonment. Maybe only an uninhibited following of our desire to know the truth can bring us into genuine encounter with depth, future, freedom and beauty.

And yet we may already have given up the quest for truth, saying to ourselves: "There is no final truth; truth is relative to each person's subjective preferences; truth is a useful social convention; truth cannot be found." If we have been tempted to such conclusions, we may perhaps take comfort in the fact that some famous philosophers have also taught these same "truths." But we must also note that other great minds, most of them in fact, have demonstrated the self-contradiction in such dogmas.

Suppose, for example, someone says that it is not possible to know the truth. This translates into: "It is a *truth* that it is not possible to know the truth." Such a statement is self-contradictory because it appeals to our capacity to know the truth (at least the truth of the above statement) even in the act of denying that we have such a capacity. It overlooks the fact that we implicitly appeal to our trust in the truth every time we raise a doubt about something or every time we say: "It is the case that such and such is so." We could never hope to convince others even that relativism is a truthful philosophical position unless we assumed in advance that these others were capable of recognizing the "truth" of our skepticism. Hence, even if we may at times have explicitly despaired of ever finding the truth, we have not been able to eradicate either our desire for it or our implicit appeal to criteria of truth every time we use the verb "to be."

Every act of judging or of questioning presupposes the possibility of our finding the truth. Without an implicit "faith" that intelligibility and truth can be found we would not have the courage either to seek understanding or to make judgments about the world around us. If deep within us some cynical voice dominated our consciousness by saying "there is no intelligibility or truth to be found in the world or yourself," then we would never even so much as ask a question. Yet by the fact that we do ask questions and make judgments (even, for example, "it is a *truth* that there *is* no intelligibility or truth") we give ample evidence that we cannot eradicate our primordial trust in the intelligibility and truth of reality. Like it or not, we are irremediably tied to truth—even as we take flight from it. We have already seen that the same applies to our relation to depth, futurity, freedom and beauty.

I stated earlier that the direct evidence for the fact of your having a desire to know lies in the simple fact that you find yourself spontaneously asking questions. If you find yourself questioning this, then it is because you have a desire to know. Or if you are asking what the meaning of these peculiar reflections is, or if there is any truth to them, then this spontaneous questioning is evidence of your own desire to know. You have a desire to know the truth, and it sharply reveals itself in your asking of simple questions.[2]

But there are different types of questions. Some of our questions inquire as to what a thing is or ask about its meaning, intelligibility or significance. This type of questioning is resolved when we are given an "insight" into the essence of something. If you find yourself asking what the author of this book is trying to get across in these sentences, then this is an example of the first type of question. It may be called a "question for understanding." It will reach its goal when you find yourself saying: "Aha, I now see the point."

But the gaining of understanding is not the end of the questioning process. For not every insight is in touch with reality. There can be illusory along with realistic understanding. So a second type of question spontaneously arises, and it leads you to ask whether your insights or those of others are *true*. For example, in reading this chapter, if you reach the point of saying, "I see the point the author is trying to make," an uneasiness will eventually emerge that will be given expression in this fashion: "Yes, I see the point, but is the point well taken? Is it faithful to the facts of my own experience? Is it based in reality? Is it true?" This type of questioning provides evidence that you are not content with mere insight and understanding. You want *truthful* insight and *correct* understanding. Thus you ask: Is it *really* so? Does this or that viewpoint correspond with *reality*? Is it a fact?

We may call this second type a "question for reflection" or simply a "critical question." It is especially our critical questions that give evidence of our desire to know and of our fundamental discontent with mere understanding. We want to make sure that our insights, hypotheses and theories are true to reality. Otherwise we remain unsatisfied with them. This restlessness in the face of mere "thinking" leads us to undertake "verificational" experiments in order to test whether our insight and understanding fit the real world or whether perhaps they are out of touch with reality. Our discontent with mere thinking, no matter how ingenious such thinking may be, is what leads us toward "knowledge." Our sense that knowing is more significant than simply thinking is the result of our allowing ourselves to be motivated by a "desire to know."[3]

We have all had the experience of listening to very clever people and of reading very learned books. We often assume that their brilliance amounts to veracity, and so sometimes we fail to raise further questions about them. It is very easy to be overwhelmed by the genius of an argument or the brightness of an idea. But if our critical sense is sufficiently awakened we realize, as Bernard Lonergan puts it, that "not every bright idea is a true idea." There is always the need to ask whether "bright ideas" are in touch with reality. We must heed the imperative in our mind that tells us: "Be critical; do not settle for mere understanding." Science is perhaps the most obvious example of this need to challenge hypothetical insight with critical questions.

Again, it takes only a little reflection on our own experience to notice how difficult it can be at times to follow this critical imperative and to wean ourselves away from fallacious or shallow understanding. This is the case with respect to our knowledge of others and of reality in general but especially with respect to self-knowledge. Because the desire to know is not the only motivation, and perhaps not even the dominant one, in our conscious lives at any given time, we may easily allow some other impulse to construct self-images that have little to do with what we really are. And we may find these fictitious self-images so appealing to our desire for power, gratification or approval that they divert us from attaining appropriate insight into ourselves.

Our propensity for self-deception is one of the most interesting and most philosophically troubling characteristics of our human nature. Why should conscious beings whose questions constantly reveal the fact of an underlying desire to know as an ineradicable aspect of their consciousness also have such a tendency to repress this desire to know when it seeks self-knowledge?

At least part of the reason for the flight from insight into ourselves lies in the fact that, in addition to having an ineradicable desire to know, we also need acceptance and approval. And it appears at times that we will pay almost any price to be held in high positive regard by significant others. We will go to the point of denying even to ourselves those aspects of our lives and characters that we suspect might not be approved of by others. And so we will hide these "unacceptable" features not only from them but from ourselves as well. Self-deception occurs when, in trying to fulfill criteria of worth established by our immediate social environment, some part of us simply fails to live up to its standards. Rather than admit the presence in us of an "unsocialized" component we often deny its presence and pretend that we fit comfortably within the circle drawn by familial, national, academic, ecclesiastical or other societal conditions of self-esteem. The "unacceptable" side of ourselves does not simply go away, however, and our latent interest in the truth feebly attempts to bring it into explicit recognition. But our need for immediate approval provokes us to take strong internal measures to keep it out of explicit consciousness. Thus our pure desire to know comes into conflict with our desire for acceptance when the area of knowledge to be explored is that of the self in the context of social conditions of personal value. This divided condition makes us wonder, then, whether we can find truth at all without giving up our desire for approval by others.

Are these two desires—the desire for acceptance and the desire for truth—condemned to perpetual mutual combat, or is there not some way in which they can be reconciled? Is there any sense in which the need to be loved can co-exist with our need to know the truth?

Some philosophers, both ancient and modern, have despaired of such a union. They tell us that if we honestly follow our desire for the truth we will have to admit that ultimately reality as such is either hostile or indifferent to us. They point especially to the facts of suffering and death as evidence that, in the final analysis, we are not cared for.[4] They admit that we have a powerful longing for affection and love, but they advise us to reach some compromise between the demand for acceptance and the ultimate opaqueness of "reality" to any such desire. This view may be called "absurdist" since it sees an irrational flaw at the heart of reality dividing it dualistically into two incommensurable elements: human consciousness with its desire for acceptance on the one side, and the universe with its refusal to satisfy this desire on the other. The incongruity of these two sides of reality, namely man and the universe, means that reality as a whole does not make sense. It is absurd.[5]

One must question, then, whether our deep need for a sense of self-worth can ever be satisfied as long as our sense of reality is an absurdist one. And, one must also ask, can our desire to know ever really emerge as the dominant motivational force in our lives if we truly believe that the universe is, in its depths, unaccepting toward us? The absurdist reply is that the hostility of the universe toward us is the occasion for our exercising an honesty and courage that will give us an even deeper sense of self-esteem than we could have in a beneficent universe. Facing the challenge of living without hope requires heroism, and, therefore, it allows us to feel better about ourselves to the extent that we face courageously the insurmountable challenge of an absurd universe. Thus, in order for us to be honest about ourselves there is no need for an ultimate or transcendent context of love. All we need is to summon up from within ourselves the courage to "face the facts."

The tragic or absurdist interpretation which holds that our courage comes only from "within" us is a position which promotes itself as the only honest interpretation of the facts of human existence. Its apparent heroism and honesty has made the tragic vision an attractive one for at least some people for centuries. On the surface it seems to be an exemplary instance of following the desire for truth, no matter how much it hurts. At first sight this "tragic" interpretation appears to avoid self-deception and to face the truth by renouncing the need for love, approval and acceptance. The self can stand on its own in complete lucidity about its situation in the world, without the support of the universe or even of other people.

And yet, on closer examination, the tragic alternative, in its denying the basic dependency and interdependency of all things, is itself also conducive to self-deception. It seems to fall short of complete honesty inasmuch as it fails to acknowledge the necessity of sources of courage beyond the individual's own heroism. The tragic hero who announces the absurdity of the world stands up courageously against the alleged hostility of the universe or society, and this often explains the appeal tragic heroes have to the rebellious tendencies within us. But the absurdist hero is oblivious to the sustenance our courage receives from our environment, and this is where a certain dishonesty begins.

It is simply not the case that any of us as individuals can autonomously ground our own courage. We are all organically tied into the universe at many levels, physical, chemical, biological, psychological, and social. Our organic interdependence with nature and other persons renders suspect the view that "I" alone am the sole source of my courage and that the universe is fundamentally against me. None of us lives in such splendid isolation or without the cooperation of many levels of interdependency and without many vital connections to the environment that sustains us. The courage that gives us a sense of self-worth is derived from our (usually unconscious) participation in proximate power sources or "transference objects" which are grounded in other sources beyond themselves. Complete honesty requires the acknowledgment of all the sources of power that energize our courage.

Tragic thinking, attractive as it may be in its call to heroism, does not fully advert to the natural and social (let alone transcendent) environmental conditions involved in rendering heroism possible in the first place. Hence I do not think that the tragic or absurdist vision resolves our problem as to whether the need to be loved can co-exist with the need to be honest. For there seems to be a basic element of insincerity, or at least a lack of lucidity, in the tragic or absurdist vision of human existence.

Is there, then, any rationally conceivable way in which our desire for truth could co-exist with and even support our desire to be accepted and loved? Or must we instead accept the tragic compromise as the best one available?

Let me propose another hypothetical response to our problem. Suppose that in the deepest depths of reality, in its dimension of futurity, at the ultimate horizon of our quest for freedom, beauty and truth there lies an acceptance, an approval, a love that is *unconditional*, one that places no conditions of worth upon us but offers complete acceptance regardless of whether or not we have fulfilled any such criteria in our actions or in our characters. Suppose that the ultimate environment of our lives, as distinct from our immediate social and natural habitats, is unconditional love. If there is such an ultimately loving dimension to reality, would it not make possible a resolution of our dilemma? Would it not be an acceptance that embraces every aspect of ourselves, including those that seem to be unacceptable to our immediate social environment?

If we thought of ourselves as existing within the context of an acceptance that places no conditions of worth upon us in order to approve and affirm us in our existence, would we have the need to hide anything from ourselves? Would we require the mask of self-deception in order to win the acceptance we long for? Such a context would undercut the need for a self-deception based on the obsession with approval by others. For the positive regard which we seek would be bestowed on us in any case. We would not be required to live up to any particular standards of cultural expectation in order to have the acceptance and love we seek. In such a hypothetical environment our self-esteem would be a gift and not something we would have to earn. In such a context self-deception would not be necessary since we would not have to strive to fulfill impossible conditions for being loved. Nor would any tragic compromise between the need for acceptance and the desire for the truth be necessary. Both exigencies would be satisfied simultaneously.

But is there such an environment? Or is not this hypothesis a prime example of our love of illusions and our aversion to the hard truth about the universe and ourselves?

This hypothesis of an unconditionally accepting ultimate context of our lives is one response (a specifically religious one) to our perennial and irrepressible questions for understanding: What is reality like? What kind of universe are we dealing with? What is the essence of things? The "hypothesis" of an unconditionally loving depth dimension to reality is a clear alternative to the tragic insight that reality is absurd. But as we have seen, our desire to know is not satisfied with mere insights or hypotheses. Hence it raises a second, critical type of question that seeks to verify whether reality does correspond after all to our hypothetical models, or whether perhaps the latter are just nice ideas with no relation to reality whatsoever. When presented with the "hypothesis" that the depth of reality is unconditional love, our desire to know the truth will immediately raise the reflective question: Is unconditional love a reality, or is it not perhaps an illusion invented out of our deep desire for approval, and projected onto an indifferent universe? Is it rational for us to commit ourselves to the religious "hypothesis" (if I may be permitted to use this crude and inadequate term) that we are unconditionally loved? In other words does such a commitment contradict or correspond with our ineradicable desire for the truth? Granted that it would be nice if we lived in such a trustworthy universe circumscribed by unbounded love. But we cannot help asking whether all this would be too good to be true.

Any attempt to arbitrate this issue as though it were just one more question for scientific or logical inquiry would obviously be silly. We simply cannot get our limited minds around the totality whose ultimate nature we are attempting to understand and of which our minds are themselves after all only a part. An attempt by a part to comprehend the totality of which it is a part is destined for frustration. So in striving to know whether the "hypothesis" of unconditional love corresponds with reality we have to seek an avenue other than such direct verification.

I think we have an "indirect" way of testing the truth-status of the religious trust in unconditional acceptance. We may ask whether a trust that we are unconditionally loved promotes or frustrates our desire to know which is itself utterly intolerant of illusions and whose only interest is the truth. The deepest criterion of truth, as we have seen, is fidelity to our desire to know. Thus we may each simply ask whether our trusting that the depth of reality is unconditionally accepting of us is an attitude that fosters our desire to know or whether perhaps it impedes this basic desire's innate intention of truth. If this trust encourages our desire to cut through illusions about ourselves, others and the universe, then it is faithful to the desire to know and therefore fulfills our essential criterion of truth (which is fidelity to the desire to know). If, on the other hand, we become convinced that this kind of trust is an impediment to the free flow of our desire for the truth, then we may repudiate such trust as itself illusory, as unfaithful to our desire to know. This, however, is a kind of indirect verification that each person must undertake for himself or herself alone.

For my part I would argue that a trust in our "supposed" ultimate environment of unconditional acceptance would liberate rather than conflict with a desire for the truth and would therefore be consistent with rationality (if by rationality we mean the state of following our desire to know even when other desires tempt us away from the truth). The belief that the universe in its depths is ultimately loving is a portrait of reality fully congruous with and supportive of the desire to know, and is therefore a truthful position for consciousness to take. Indeed I would go so far as to insist that it is the *only* hypothetical matrix that can fully support our desire to know as it seeks to disentangle itself from other desires and the strong temptation to self-deception. Could a trust that nurtures the desire to know (which by definition cannot settle for illusions) possibly be in conflict with this same desire? This is the philosophical question I would like the reader to ponder. In other words, could our trust in an ultimate horizon of unconditional love possibly be illusory if such trust fosters the interests of our passion for the truth by eliminating the need for a self-deception that in turn causes us to distort our understanding of others and reality as such?

The only alternative to a religious vision of ultimate unconditional acceptance is the view that reality offers us merely conditional acceptance at best. But can this latter option conceivably be a truthful interpretation of our situation? Our settling for merely conditional love, a love whose other side is always fear of rejection if one does not fulfill the conditions, lies in opposition to a desire for the truth about ourselves. For in such a case we shall inevitably devise illusory conceptions of ourselves in order to combat the fear of rejection by others who place conditions on their acceptance of us. The desire for unconditional love, though, coincides with our (perhaps repressed) desire for the truth about ourselves. And if we could be truthful about ourselves the chances are good that we would be more truthful in our understanding of others and of the world as such.

Therefore, the hypothesis of a universe grounded in unconditional love need not be viewed as a projection. Instead the "tragic" view that the universe is really hostile toward us may itself be interpreted as a projection rooted in a distorted, unrealistic perception of ourselves as ultimately unloved. On the other hand, a commitment to the vision that the ultimate environment of our existence is unconditionally accepting can encourage our desire for the truth and thereby remove our temptation to settle for illusory projection. Without such a trust, given the power of our drive for approval, our desire for the truth will be repressed whenever we advert to traits of our characters that seem unapprovable.

In Jean-Paul Sartre's play *No Exit* there are three characters confined to an enclosed "hell" where their punishment consists of having their lives and past actions painfully exposed to the others. They each attempt in "bad faith" to hide the truth about their deeds and lives not only from the other two but from themselves as well. The play is an impressive philosophical and dramatic presentation of the human tendency to self-deception and of the pain involved in self-disclosure. By the end of the play the characters are still trying to cover up their real identities by burying themselves in the superficial approval of one of the others. But the presence of the third party painfully intrudes and shatters these attempted liaisons based on self-deception. The presence of other people thus constitutes a "hell" from which there is no exit.

Sartre's play, like his philosophy as a whole, speaks eloquently of the futility of self-deception. But neither the play nor the tragic philosophy offers any "solution" to this universal human problem of "bad faith." One cannot help but notice throughout *No Exit*, for example, the complete absence of any inkling of unconditional acceptance that alone would allow for the emergence of truthfulness about oneself. When one character "accepts" the other it is only a superficial part and not the whole of the person that wins approval. And, as we may easily observe from our own experience, it is the feeling that one is accepted only in part and not as a whole that leads us to self-deception in the first place. We should seriously examine, therefore, the possibility that the desire for truth, beginning with the truth about oneself, is simultaneously the search for an environment of unconditional acceptance in which one will feel at ease to acknowledge *all* aspects of one's life and identity.

It is axiomatic that a distorted sense of ourselves is likely to result in our misconstruing the identities of others and of the nature of reality as a whole. If this axiom needs "empirical" support we can readily find it in psychology. Diagnoses of psychic illness and of a person's inability to relate to others or to "reality" usually point to the patient's distorted sense of his or her own self as the root of the illness. And the restoration of a reality sense must begin by a removal of the patient's own self-misperception. It is not an accident that this removal takes place only when the patient learns self-acceptance. Nor is it mere coincidence that self-acceptance occurs most readily when the patient is placed in a therapeutic situation that allows him or her to retrieve sides of the self that had been repressed out of fear of disapproval by an earlier and narrower social setting. It follows that the eviction of self-deception would open us up to a more truthful relationship to others and to the universe. When the distortive filter that we have constructed in our efforts to bury dimensions of our own identity is dissolved we can then see more clearly into other people and into our whole world. Thus the "truth" about reality as such becomes more transparent to us when the veils of untruth are taken away from self-awareness.

As we saw in Chapter 3, our desire for unconditional (infinite) approval is usually projected onto near-at-hand transference objects that we hope will give us the fulfillment we seek. And we also pointed out the ultimately disappointing nature of these transference affairs. We can now specify more precisely the root of the disillusionment. It consists simply of the failure of our transference objects to give us the unconditional acceptance that we need in order to find the truth. The disappointment at bottom is that of not being in a proper relation to the truth. But only an environment of unconditional acceptance can establish the context for this relationship. Hence it seems to me that a fidelity to the desire to know, that is, a fundamental truthfulness is supported by a trusting commitment to our "hypothesis." And in experiencing the intimate connection between trust in unconditional love and the liberation of one's desire to know from unnecessary illusions about oneself and the universe we have an indirect "verification" of the truthfulness of the"hypothesis."

These observations, therefore, should lead us to take a closer look at the possible "truth" value of those religious faiths which maintain that our lives are indeed encircled by an ultimate environment of unconditional love. It should also alert us to elements in these same traditions that seem to proclaim an "ultimate" that is only conditionally accepting.

As I have attempted to reason, the conviction of being unconditionally loved could be called truthful because it nurtures the one desire in us that seeks the truth. It fosters and encourages our desire to know. In the spirit of the religious conviction that perfect love casts out fear, it allows this desire first to penetrate and retrieve areas of the self that had been hidden in fear. The sense of being unconditionally loved dissolves the usual terror that accompanies our desires, and it releases the human passion to seek the truth which alone brings true freedom. A sense of being unconditionally loved liberates the core of human *eros* by conquering the fear that usually diverts it into blind alleys of frustration. A sense of being unconditionally loved sets free our desire to know so that it can pursue its unrestricted goal, the truth. I would conclude, then, that the quest for unconditional love is also a quest for the truth and by no means an illusory escape from reality.

The name for this truth that coincides with unconditional love is God. That truth is what the word "God" means. And if that word has not much meaning for you, translate it and speak of the ultimate objective of your desire to know. Perhaps in order to do this you must forget many things that you have learned about God, perhaps even that word itself. For if you know that God means *truth* your affirmation of this ultimate horizon cannot, by definition, be an illusion. For the desire for the truth undercuts all illusions. If you identify "God" with the unrestricted horizon of truth and love toward which your desire to know is directed, you need not fear that your belief is a projection of wishful thinking. If the desire for God is at root the desire for truth, then this desire will not be able to take refuge in illusions or mere thinking. The desire for God coincides with our desire for truth. A fifth way to think about God, therefore, is to think of the horizon of truth which continually activates our desire to ask questions and allows us no peace until we have surrendered to it.

One final remark about this truth which is the objective of all our questioning. Truth is ultimately a *mysterium tremendum et fascinans.* As in the case of the "sacred," we both hide from it and seek it at the same time. We know that the truth hurts, but we also intuit that it alone can provide a firm foundation to our lives. I have suggested here that the ultimate truth, depth, future, freedom and beauty into whose embrace we are constantly invited consists of an unconditional love. And it is perhaps this love that is the *tremendum* from which we flee as well as the *fascinans* that promises us ultimate fulfillment. Is it possible that our flight from depth, futurity, freedom, beauty and truth is, in the final analysis, a flight from love?

The Absence of God

The very notion of desire implies the lack or absence of that which is desired. If we actually possessed what we desire we could not desire it. Having something eliminates the longing for it. At the same time, however, we could not desire something unless its presence were already "on the horizon," so to speak. If it were totally and in every sense beyond apprehension we could not long for it at all. In some way desire is activated by the *presence* to us of that absence which we desire.

This paradox of suspension between having and not having is the very condition that makes it possible for us to ask questions and to seek the truth. Asking a question is possible because we do not yet know the answer. If we knew the answer we would not ask the question in the first place. And yet we have to know something about what we are questioning in order to ask about it at all. The truth our question is seeking has to be "absent" in order for us to seek it. But at the same time our consciousness has to dwell within the horizon of truth in order for us to inquire about it at all. In other words, our minds must already have moved into a specific field of knowledge and been influenced by the objects in this field in order for us to ask about what lies within the horizon. For example, I could not seriously ask whether a specific equation were correctly formulated unless my mind had already moved into the horizon of mathematics. And I would not be interested in asking whether Einstein's theories are realistic unless I had already been influenced at least to some degree by the field of modern physics.

Nor could I seriously desire the truth about myself, others and the world unless the horizon of truth had already encircled my consciousness. The fact that the truth does not force itself upon us, that it does not coerce our consciousness, is rich with implications for the troubling question raised by both believers and unbelievers as to why God seems to be so absent and inobvious in terms of our ordinary experience. For if we are identifying the divine with Truth, a simple reflection on our relationship to truth can help us to understand and "tolerate" the absence of God. The "absence" of the truth, its unobtrusiveness, is a necessary absence if it is to function as the criterion of our knowledge. If we are to be nurtured by the truth rather than subjecting it to the caprice of our own whimsy, then we must allow the truth to be an horizon that comprehends us rather than a set of objects over which we can set ourselves up as masters. Another way of saying this is that we must subordinate our desire for power, and any other wayward wishings, to our desire to know the truth. For the latter desire is essentially a longing not to possess but to be possessed by the realm of the true. It is ultimately a desire for a union whose best metaphor is interpersonal love. This means that we should not attempt to make the truth completely "present." The obsession with absolute "presence" is at root a will to control. The truth, if it is to remain the truth and not a possession, cannot be controlled or manipulated into becoming totally manifest in the narrow confines of the present. If we find the elusiveness, depth or "futurity" of truth intolerable, it may be because our strong impulse to master takes precedence over our desire to be grasped by the truth.

If we have appropriately identified God with truth, this may help us to accept the inevitable absence of God from the realm of things that can be possessed.

Religion

Religion may be understood, then, as the conscious decision to move within the truth. It is a rejection of the strong temptation to make truth the object of our will to mastery. It is a surrender to truth as the *mysterium tremendum et fascinans* in which alone our freedom and fulfillment lie. Religion is an ongoing conversion to the dimension of the true that transcends the everyday world of fear and all the illusions based on fear. Wherever there is a sincere desire for the truth about ourselves, others and the world there is authentic religion, even if it does not go by that name. The religiousness of this desire for the truth consists of a fundamental trust in the ultimate intelligibility of reality without which we would not have the courage to ask questions and to seek the truth. Such trust in the intelligibility of reality is given symbolic expression in the specific religious traditions, and these symbols have the function of fortifying our fundamental trust in reality's intelligibility. Because we are constantly confronted by absurdities that tempt us to distrust, we have a constant and compelling need to have our capacity for trust restored to us. It is the purpose of "religions" to re-present symbolically the trust-worthiness of reality,[6] and to repair our fractured confidence in the intelligibility of reality. By virtue of this restoration religion promotes the interests of our desire to know. The latter simply cannot adventurously pursue its objective in the absence of a core conviction that the universe is intelligible.

We may even go so far as to say that religion, from the perspective of human consciousness and longing, has its origins essentially in the desire for the truth. This is not to deny, of course, that concrete religious life is ambiguously overlaid with imaginings rooted in our many other desires as well, and that there are "wishings" in all religious people that interfere with the pure desire for the truth. It may even be that what often passes for religion in the perspective of social science is quite contrary to the normative portrait I am painting here. But I would still insist that *essentially* religion originates in the desire to know. The core of religion is an uncompromising passion for the truth.

Such a view of religion is, of course, at odds with the one often described in the writings of psychologists, historians, sociologists and philosophers who have criticized it as an illusion. However, I am speaking here of what I consider to be essential to religion and not of its accidental perversions. No doubt the critics are correct in their negative evaluations of what they consider to be religion. For there is indeed much childish manipulation and infantile desire underlying the illusions in much actual religious life. But beneath these accidental deviations the core of religious consciousness is, as Whitehead puts it, a "penetrating sincerity." And it has been my objective in this book to present only essential elements of religion, and deliberately to avoid dwelling on its darker side.

Conclusion:
Mystery

The most important way of responding to the question "What is God?" is of course to say that essentially God is *mystery*. For many believers the term "mystery" is resonant with the depth, future, freedom, beauty and truth to which I have pointed in this book. And undoubtedly for many such individuals the term "mystery" is more religiously appropriate than any of the five notions I have used. Rudolf Otto considered *mysterium* to be the very essence of the sacred, and theological reflection may no more casually abandon use of the term "mystery" than the word "God." The notion of mystery is indispensable to our discourse about the divine.

Therefore, we must come back to this word "mystery" at the end of our obviously unsatisfactory attempts to verbalize the "whatness" of God. To say that God is ultimately mystery is the final word in any proper thinking about the divine. Recourse to the notion of "mystery" is essential in order to accentuate the utter inadequacy of any thoughts we may formulate about God. And it is also necessary to evoke in us a cognitive "feeling" of the inexhaustibility we have pointed to by way of our five metaphors.

None of the five notions I have employed can be substituted for that of mystery. My objective in resorting provisionally to them has been simply to provide several avenues leading up to the idea of mystery as the most
appropriate designation for the divine. In the esoteric language of theology, it might be said that my purpose in writing this little book has been to provide a simple "mystagogy," that is, an "introduction to mystery."[1] We live in
an age and culture in which there reigns an "eclipse of mystery." And the difficulty people have in connecting their
experience with the word "God" is for the most part a consequence of the lack of a sense of mystery in their lives.[2]
Mystagogy would not be necessary if we could presume
that people were universally in touch with the encompassing horizon of mystery in their lives and in the world
around them. Books on the problem of God would not be
so abundant if mystery were self-evident in our cultural
experience. For ultimately "God" means mystery, and the
prevalence of a sense of mystery would render books like
this one superfluous.

Unfortunately the dimension of mystery, though never
absent from the experience of any of us, has been lost sight
of by our theoretical consciousness. It still hovers around
the fringes of our spontaneous involvements in life, in our
relations to nature, other persons and ourselves. And it is
intimated in the symbols and stories that inform our consciousness. But in a world where the mastering methods
and techniques of science have become so dominant the
cognitive surrender that a sense of mystery requires of us
has often been subordinated to an "epistemology of control."[3] That is, the handing of ourselves over to mystery has
become almost impossible whenever knowledge has been
understood in terms of power. Confrontation with the
uncontrollable domain of mystery often leaves us feeling

insecure, restless and even hostile. So we strive to suppress the unmanageable horizon of mystery and vanquish the need for any surrender of self to it.

In the face of this eclipse of mystery the very possibility of speaking meaningfully about God has likewise diminished, even to the point of almost vanishing. And yet mystery cannot be completely suppressed. It still functions as the silent horizon that makes all of our experience and knowledge possible in the first place. In its humility and unobtrusiveness it refuses to force itself upon us, but nonetheless it graciously undergirds our existence and understanding without making itself obvious. We go through the course of our lives enabled by the horizon of mystery to think, to inquire, to adventure and discover, but we seldom become explicitly aware of its encompassing presence-in-absence or extend our gratitude to it for giving us the free space in which to live our lives. My objective in the preceding has been to render this dimension of mystery somewhat more obvious by leading up to it with alternative names. But because of its highly theoretical nature such an approximation still leaves us only at the doorway of mystery. Only the actual living of our lives and not the mere reading of a book can lead us into the realm of mystery. The most that any book like this can do is merely point the reader in a certain direction. It cannot substitute for experience itself.

A theoretical introduction to mystery may not be a necessity to many people for whom the term already possesses a symbolic power sufficiently expansive to open up to them the ultimate horizon of their existence. But for countless others the term "mystery," like the words "God" and "sacred," has also lost its power and meaning, or has become so trivialized by common usage that it no longer evokes in them any deep sense of the inexhaustible depths of reality. For some the notion of mystery has even become altogether empty. For that reason it is essential today to provide a sort of pedagogy to mystery. I do not in any way consider my own attempts adequate, and I have presented them only as starting points for introducing some small part of what is designated theologically by the notion of divine mystery. At this point, then, it may be well to speak a bit more directly about the word "mystery" as such, if indeed this term is finally the most suitable one we can use in thinking of God.

Mystery and Problem

The term "mystery" is often misunderstood simply as a gap in our knowledge, a temporary hiatus that might possibly be closed as scientific consciousness advances further. According to this narrow view, as our intellectual mastery of the world progresses we will find answers to the "mysteries" which remain in principle answerable but in fact unanswered at the present. Thus the realm of "mystery" will allegedly be gradually diminished, and "knowledge" will take its place. As a noted psychologist has put it, the objective of science is to eliminate mystery.[4]

When "mystery" is understood in this fashion, namely as a gap to be replaced by scientific knowledge, it is little wonder that the word no longer functions to evoke a religious sense of the *tremendum et fascinans*. For in this case "mystery" is merely a vacuum that begs to be filled with our intellectual achievements and not an ineffable depth summoning us to surrender ourselves completely to it. If such is the meaning of mystery, then it is hardly adequate as a term for the divine.

But the gaps in our present understanding and knowledge would better be called *problems* than mysteries.[5]

"Problem" points to an area of ignorance that is able eventually to be solved by the application of human ingenuity. Perhaps at the present time a "problem" remains unsolved and even unsolvable by the devices at our disposal, but it should not be called a mystery, for it is at least open to some sort of future solution. For example, a science that connects gravitational, electromagnetic and other forces into a unified field theory is at present unavailable. But since such a science will probably emerge at some future time it is better to call this quandary a problem than a mystery. A problem is in principle open to a scientific, logical or technological solution. It is somehow under our human control and can be mastered by our intellectual or technological powers.

Mystery, on the other hand, denotes a region of reality that, instead of growing smaller as we grow wiser and more powerful, can actually be experienced as growing larger and more incomprehensible as we solve more of our scientific and other problems. It is the region of the "known unknown," the horizon that keeps expanding and receding into the distance the more our knowledge advances. It is the arena of the incomprehensible and unspeakable that makes us aware of our ignorance, of how much more there yet remains to be known. No one to date has shown Socrates to be wrong in his insistence that we are truly wise only when we are aware of the abysmal poverty of our present cognitional achievements. Such an awareness of the lowliness of our knowledge is possible, though, only if we have already been made aware of the inexhaustibility of the yet-to-be-known, that is, of mystery. It is wise for us to emphasize that this state of "learned ignorance" *(docta ignorantia)* is possible only to those whose horizons have expanded beyond the ordinary, in other words, to those who have begun to taste the mysteriousness of reality.

Mystery, in contrast to problems, is incapable of any

"solution." Whereas problems can be solved and thus gotten out of the way, mystery becomes more prominent the deeper our questions go and the surer our answers become. Mystery appears to consciousness at the "limit" of our ordinary problem-oriented questions. It reveals itself decisively at the point where we seriously ask what may be called "limit-questions," questions that lie at the "boundary" of our ordinary problem-solving consciousness.[6] For example, while science is dominated by problems for which some resolution or definitive answer is expected, the scientist might find himself or herself eventually asking: Why should I do science at all? Why search for intelligibility in the universe? Is the universe completely intelligible, as scientific questioning seems to take for granted? At this point the scientist has reached the limit of problem and has asked a kind of question that explicitly opens up the horizon of mystery. This type may be called limit-questioning since it does not fall within, but rather only *at*, the boundary of ordinary scientific inquiry.

To give another example: the field of ethics attempts to give answers to our moral dilemmas, but at the limits of ethical investigation there arise such questions as: Why bother about ethics at all? Why be responsible? Why pursue the good life? Ethicians might engage in endless problem-solving exercises trying to decide whether this or that action on the part of a spouse constitutes fidelity or infidelity. But at a certain point the following questions may arise: Why should we be faithful at all? Why keep promises? Is the universe at heart faithful and trustworthy? If it is not, then why should I worry about fidelity and promise-keeping? At this juncture we have shifted from ethical problems into the realm of the mysterious and unsolvable. Ethics can no more easily answer these limiting questions than science can tell us why we should seek intelligibility in the universe.

Another illustration: literary criticism attempts to respond to questions concerning whether this or that work of literature is aesthetically worthy of our respect. But at the limit of literary criticism there arise questions that it cannot itself address: Why pursue the beautiful? Why bother about aesthetic criteria at all? What is beauty? Again we have moved out of problem and into mystery.

Still another example: politics and other social sciences raise questions about how we can best prepare for our future life together on this planet. But they cannot respond by themselves to the limit-question: What is the future? Why should we bother about the future at all?

Finally: logic raises questions of a problematic nature as to whether this or that proposition follows logically from its premises. But at the limits of logic there arise questions to which logic alone is inadequate: Why bother about being logical at all? Why pursue the truth? What is reality like that we simply assume that we should be rational in our approach to it? If reality were absurd, would there be any point in being logical or rational?

Each discipline is specified by the types of questions it raises, the kinds of problems with which it deals. It pursues its questions with a degree of success proportionate to the problems it solves. But at the boundaries of all the various fields of human inquiry we come to an impasse that we cannot get beyond no matter how much intellectual effort we exert. Our problem-solving techniques cannot get us over the encompassing horizon of mystery opened up by our limit-questions.

The place of mystery, and hence the appropriate place for the introduction of a specifically religious discourse, is at the limits of our problem-oriented questioning, when our inquiry shifts to another key entirely. At such a point we realize we are asking questions that no human ingenuity will ever solve or "remove." But even though we cannot give final solutions to these impossible questions we may still respond (that is, "answer back") to them. This response is appropriately not one of trying to ignore, repress or eliminate them, but rather allowing them to take over our consciousness and pull us into the mystery that lurks on the other side of our problems. The very fact of our asking limit-questions implies that the horizon of mystery has already taken hold of our consciousness. The horizon of mystery addresses us from the other side of our limit-questions and draws us beyond the merely problematic. And we show our proclivity for mystery whenever we find ourselves asking limit-questions. Conversely, the refusal ever to be concerned about these unanswerable questions is perhaps the result of a repression of mystery which a culture built predominantly on the ideal of power inevitably promotes.

In addition to the mysterious questions that arise at the limits of our intellectual life there are also the "boundary experiences" that confront us at the edges of our everyday life. The encounter with suffering, frustration and ultimately death arouses questions of an entirely different sort from those we "normally" ask. Marginal experiences interrupt the normal course of human existence and let the never completely absent dimension of mystery enter more explicitly into our consciousness. Usually we are preoccupied with the ordinary "problems" of life, such as how to acquire enough money to pay for tuition, how to pass a course, how to gain friends and have a gratifying social life, how to embark upon the appropriate career, etc. In other words "how" questions dominate the ordinary course of our lives. But there are certain "shipwreck" or "earthquake" experiences that occasionally break into the routine of our lives, and when they do we experience the superficiality of our pragmatic "how" questions and the invasion of "why" or "ultimate" questions. Such shipwreck experiences raise questions that stand at the "limit" of our ordinary consciousness of life, and they can sensitize us in an extraordinary way to the mystery that always silently accompanies and encompasses our lives. When we are beset by these marginal experiences we ask "ultimate" questions more intently perhaps than before. Can this be all there is to life? Are tragedy and death the final word? Is there any final meaning to my work? Is there an answer to the problem of suffering? Perhaps more often than not it is the questions aroused by tragedy that make us most vulnerable to the touch of mystery.

And yet it would be a mistake to say that the awakening to a sense of mystery is inevitably contingent upon the shock of negative experiences that jolt us out of our everyday insensitivity. For positive and ecstatic moments of deep joy can just as readily transport us beyond the boundary of pedestrian existence. Many people testify to "peak-experiences" that have introduced them to mystery much more decisively than has any experience of the negative side of life. The feeling of being deeply loved by another person or of being enthralled by great beauty can also lead us to ask limit-questions. Will love prevail? Is beauty only an illusion? Why cannot great moments last forever? Is there not something eternal about joy, even though my experience of it is only occasional and ephemeral? Questions such as these may dramatically open us to mystery and tempt us to a religious interpretation of the universe.

At the "limit" of our ordinary experience and our problem-solving questions we are alerted to the nearness of mystery. We sense that it has been intimately present all along but that it has not entered deeply into our explicit awareness. In limit-experience and limit-questioning we are confronted with the opportunity of making the dimension of mystery the most important and enlivening aspect of our lives.

However, we are also always tempted, when we are brought to the limits of ordinary consciousness and experience, to take flight to the "safer" refuge of the ordinary, to turn our faces away from the *tremendum et fascinans.* We do so typically by transforming mystery into problem. This is the same maneuver that we saw earlier when speaking of our tendency to turn our unmanageable existential anxiety into manipulable objects of fear so that we can dispose of it once and for all. And the enterprise of squeezing mystery into the confines of problem is likewise essentially the same thing as channelling our native capacity for the infinite into an obsession with near-at-hand transference objects. In each case the result is not only an artificial delimiting of the world around us, it is also an unfortunate diminishment of ourselves and a denial of our fundamental dignity as beings endowed with a capacity for growth into mystery.

It is our fundamental openness to mystery that sets us apart from the animal and grounds the self-transcendent nature of our lives. It is our openness to mystery that constitutes the foundation of our freedom and liberates us from the slavery of mere normality. It is because of our capacity for mystery that we experience the uneasiness and anxiety that provoke us to move beyond the status quo and to seek more intense beauty and more depth of truth. In short, mystery is what makes a truly human life possible in the first place.

And yet our native openness to mystery is often blocked by our obsession with power or security. For this reason we need techniques, paths of enlightenment, powerful images and ideas that help us remove the obstacles that stand between our consciousness and the mystery that embraces it. And so, in order to help us retrieve and respond to the repressed dimension of mystery, the world's various religions have come into being. Their founders have typically been individuals who are deeply troubled by the prevailing insensitivity to mystery and who have therefore taken steps to "enlighten" us about the mystery that always surrounds us but of which we ordinarily take little notice. Their objective is to expand our consciousness by challenging us in various ways to break out of the confines of normal, everyday consciousness. Whether by speaking in parables, walking naked through the streets of a city, posing riddles, issuing koans, prophesying, associating with outcasts, or employing any of a wide variety of awakening devices, the great religious initiators have all tried to break the hold that normality has upon us, because it is normality more than anything that covers up the mystery of life. They have thereby risked the accusation of madness by pointing to depths of reality, futurity, freedom, beauty and truth to which we are not "normally" accustomed. Their objective, however, is not to lead us away from life but more deeply into it. And apparently the only way to do so is by situating our lives and consciousness more explicitly within the realm of the mystery that they perceive in an extraordinary way.

Naming the Mystery

The question remains, however, why we may call this mystery by the name "God." Is it not sufficient that we simply have a vivid sense of the horizon of mystery? And is it essential that we give it any specific name? I think that in the case of some of us, because of the psychologically unhealthy images evoked by the word "God," it may be better not to use this word at all. There are individuals for whom the word "God" may actually stand in the way of a healthy sense of mystery. However, I would suggest that this is due less to the term itself than to faulty religious education, or trivialization through its usage in self-justifying political and ecclesiastical discourse. When the word has been so misshapen it is better to abandon it—at least until such time as its usage once again opens us to a sense of mystery.

On the other hand, the word "God" is irreplaceable in theistic religion, and it cannot be dropped completely from our Western vocabulary for naming the mysterious dimension of our existence. Furthermore, the word "God," if it is understood according to the symbolic and narrative way in which it originally came into religious consciousness, specifies and adds an element of meaning to the notion of mystery that the latter term itself may not immediately suggest. We may call this added dimension of significance simply the "graciousness" of mystery. It is in order to accentuate the gracious, self-giving nature of mystery that we use the term "God" in referring to it.[7]

We might say that there are only two major "truths" that a genuine religious sense requires.[8] All other "doctrines" of religion are derivatives of these two truths, and if we keep this in mind religion will not have to be as cumbersome or complicated an affair as it sometimes seems to be. The first of these truths, as I have been trying to show, is simply that our lives are embraced by mystery. And the second major truth is that this mystery is gracious. All religions try to give their devotees some sense of mystery, and this fact alone should be sufficient to establish a sense of community and solidarity today among all the various religious traditions, especially in the face of the contemporary suppression of mystery by cultures built on the ideal of domination. And the graciousness of mystery is also enunciated by all the religious traditions, in markedly diverse ways of course, but with a sense of unanimity that mystery is trustworthy and that our fulfillment lies only in a surrender to it. One of the most explicit formulations of the graciousness of mystery is the one which maintains that the mystery gives itself away completely, in self-emptying love, to the world which it embraces.[9] It is especially because of this graciousness that we may call the mystery by the name "God."

From these two propositions, that we are circumscribed by mystery and that this mystery, referred to as God, gives itself completely to us, can be derived all the other important ideas of religion. Religion has been made entirely too complicated and forbidding at times, and in the morass of doctrines and practices that it inevitably generates its two foundational insights may easily be lost sight of. Obviously the sense of mystery and its graciousness have to be mediated in particular forms of speech, narrative and activity corresponding to different cultural and historical habits of thought. So we must be tolerant of the diversity of religions and not seek the monotony of a homogeneous, all-encompassing religious format. But amidst the diversity of religious ideas and practices it is helpful to keep before us their common grounding in an appreciation of mystery and its gracious intimacy with the universe. Seeing through the jungle of concrete religious life to these two central tenets of religion should prevent us from making hasty condemnations of others' religious ideas and practices. For beneath their apparent peculiarity and needless extravagance there may lie a deep and simple sense of mystery and its goodness.

At the same time, however, our keeping the two "truths" constantly before us provides us with criteria to evaluate and criticize the actual religious lives of others and ourselves. For there is no doubt that religious traditions which have their origin in a decisive encounter with mystery and its graciousness can themselves deviate from their founding insights and end up participating in the eclipse of mystery. Religions can become entangled in the pursuit of domination or the legitimation of oppression and thus themselves become an obstacle to the sense of liberating mystery. Hence they should constantly be evaluated in accordance with the criteria of mystery and its graciousness.

It should not be either embarrassing or surprising to us that the human experience of the nearness and graciousness of mystery would often come to expression in a religious language heavily loaded with personalistic imagery. Although the mystery is not exhausted by its representation as a "person," the disclosure of its intimacy to human subjects endowed with intelligence, will and feelings could scarcely be possible unless it were itself presented to them as having analogously personal attributes. It is doubtful that something less than personal could inspire us deeply to trust and surrender. To persons the mystery must at least be personal itself.

It is difficult to find precise language with which to interpret the relationship of divine personality to divine mystery. Is the mystery really personal, or is personality merely one of the projective ways in which we creatively go out to meet the mystery that summons us toward itself? We have already admitted that our religions are inevitably imaginative and projective, and that there is always some level of illusion in our actual religious consciousness owing to the infantilism of desire that we can never completely eradicate. Is the propensity to think of God as personal still perhaps more a manifestation of our immaturity than a realistic appreciation of the inexhaustible mystery of reality?

Without denying that our images of a personal God always have a projective aspect to them or that these images do not exhaustively represent the mystery of our lives, we may still view "divine personality" as an indispensable symbol of the proximity to us of mystery. All of our language about this mystery necessarily has a symbolic character. Because of mystery's unavailability we cannot discuss it directly or literally. We tend to speak of it, if we speak of it at all, in terms of those places and events where it breaks through to us most decisively and intensely. For most of us the most intense disclosure of mystery probably occurs in our encounter with other persons. The child's earliest encounter with mother and father, for example, is an experience of such overwhelming "numinosity" that it remains a permanent layer of all of our involvements. And the meeting with a truly accepting and caring person is often the occasion for our experiencing the depth and graciousness of life's mystery in a decisive way. The human face itself has often been experienced as deeply mysterious, as causing us to turn away in fear or as attracting us with its enchanting power. Human personality is often the occasion for our experiencing the *mysterium tremendum et fascinans.*

Inasmuch, then, as human personality is especially transparent to the horizon of mystery and its graciousness, it is not surprising that personalist imagery would cling to our discourse about God. Since we often perceive the mystery most clearly as it shines through the lives of other persons, we can never completely separate our experience of God from the experience of personality. To do so would again be an unnecessary reduction of the mystery. The freedom and unmanipulability of other persons give us a sense of the unavailability of the mystery that is their depth. To remove the personal face of mystery is to lose access to it.

Through the medium of personality the depth of reality is "revealed" in so complete a way that we must speak of God as personal. God is the depth and ground of all personality.[10]

The Proximity of Mystery

My purpose in this book has been to suggest five ways of responding to the question "What is God?" Following the ideas of some influential modern scholars of religion, I have suggested that we may think of the "whatness" of deity in terms of the metaphor "horizon." I have bracketed the question that theists ask concerning "who" God might be in order to dwell on that aspect of the divine which cannot be expressed in personalistic categories. Thus my approach has obviously been one-sided in its emphasizing the transpersonal horizon of our lives and consciousness and in its failure to dwell for long on how God may also be thought of as a personal subject addressing us and seeking personal dialogue with us.

My approach has also been one-sided in speaking of the unavailability and even remoteness of God from the ordinary realm of experience. However, the theme of the "nearness" of the divine should also be emphasized in order to balance out that of the "absence" of God. In fact there is no contradiction between the absence and the nearness of God, and God's absence may even be understood as essential for the sake of the nearness. The unavailability of the divine is a necessary condition for the intimacy of God with the world and human persons. By not intruding into or forcing itself upon the world and personal subjects the divine mystery can be understood as caringly involved with the world. Concerned that the world not lose its integrity by being absorbed into the divine or diluted into an overbearing divine "presence," God "withdraws" from the world and persons in order to let them be. This withdrawal is not, however, an abdication but rather a selfless and humble self-distancing undertaken in order to be more involved in the world and with persons than any specific localized or objective presence would permit. The divine must withhold presence precisely in order to bestow intimacy. The self-absenting of God is essential in order to give the world its autonomy and human subjects their freedom. In this sense the absence and inobviousness of mystery may be understood as the other side of its intimacy with us.

Notes

Introduction

1. See Paul Ricoeur, *The Symbolism of Evil*, trans. by E. Buchanan (Boston: Beacon Press, 1967), p. 350.
2. Rudolf Otto, *The Idea of the Holy*, Second Edition, trans. by John W. Harvey (New York: Oxford University Press, 1950), pp. 5–11.
3. Hans-Georg Gadamer, "Articulating Transcendence," in *The Beginning and the Beyond*, ed. by Fred Lawrence (Chico, California: Scholars Press, 1984), p. 5.

Chapter 1—Depth

1. Paul Tillich, *The Shaking of the Foundations* (New York: Charles Scribner's Sons, 1948), pp. 52–63. This entire chapter is a development of ideas suggested by this important sermon of Tillich's.
2. Ibid., p. 56.
3. Ibid., p. 57.
4. On the distinction between a consolation based on the pleasure principle and the sense of a contentment beyond "consolation" see Paul Ricoeur, *The Conflict of Interpretations*, ed. by Don Ihde (Evanston: Northwestern University Press, 1974), pp. 464–67.

5. Paul Tillich develops the ideas of abyss and ground especially in his *Systematic Theology*, Vols. I & II (Chicago: University of Chicago Press, 1951, 1957).

6. See Shubert Ogden, *The Reality of God* (New York, Harper & Row, 1977), pp. 34–38.

7. Oscar Wilde, *De Profundis* (New York: Philosophical Library, 1950), p. 98.

8. Friedrich Nietzsche, *Thus Spoke Zarathustra*, trans. by Walter Kaufmann (New York: Penguin Books, 1978), pp. 156–57: "But there is something in me that I call courage, that has so far slain my every discouragement . . . . Courage also slays dizziness at the edge of abysses: and where does man not stand at the edge of abysses? Is not seeing always—seeing abysses?" (p. 157).

9. See Paul Tillich, *The Courage To Be* (New Haven: Yale University Press, 1953). I shall discuss later the question of why an "ultimate" source of courage must be posited.

10. On the distinction between focal knowledge and the tacit, inarticulate knowledge by "indwelling," see Michael Polanyi, *The Tacit Dimension* (Garden City, New York: Doubleday Anchor Books, 1967).

11. Tillich, *The Shaking of the Foundations*, p. 55.

12. Ibid. pp. 149–51.

13. Ibid. p. 55.

14. Ibid. p. 151.

Chapter 2—Future

1. See Karl Rahner, *Theological Investigations*, Vol. VI, trans. by Karl H. and Boniface Kruger (Baltimore: Helicon Press, 1969), pp. 59–68.

2. I have, of course, paraphrased Tillich here, substituting the term "future" for depth. The expression "absolute future" comes from Karl Rahner (see the preceding note).

3. See Jürgen Moltmann, *The Theology of Hope*, trans. by James W. Leitch (New York: Harper & Row, 1967), p. 16.

4. Phillip Rieff, *Fellow Teachers* (New York: Harper & Row, 1973), p. 39.
5. See Moltmann, *The Theology of Hope;* and Eulalio Baltazar, *God Within Process* (New York: Newman Press, 1970), pp. 131–51.
6. H. A. Williams, *True Resurrection* (New York: Harper Colophon Books, 1972), pp. 178–79.
7. Ibid.
8. See, for example, Moltmann, pp. 19–36.
9. For an erudite discussion of the relation between regressive and future-oriented desire see Paul Ricoeur, *Freud and Philosophy,* trans. by Denis Savage (New Haven: Yale University Press, 1970).
10. John Bowker, *The Sense of God* (Oxford: Oxford University Press, 1973), p. 151.
11. Quoted by John Bowker, *The Religious Imagination and the Sense of God* (Oxford: Oxford University Press, 1978), p. 2.
12. The analogy is liberally adapted from Bowker, *The Sense of God*, pp. 131–34.
13. Carl Raschke, *The Interruption of Eternity* (Chicago: Nelson-Hall, 1980).
14. Ibid.

Chapter 3—Freedom

1. Jean-Paul Sartre, *Existentialism and the Human Emotions,* trans. by Bernard Frectman and Hazel E. Barnes (New York: Citadel), pp. 52–59.
2. I have deliberately avoided the issue raised by determinists as to whether human freedom actually exists at all. The reason for this omission is that if freedom is essentially the horizon of our existence rather than a mere faculty or possession, then its existence cannot be argued according to the objectivist terms established by determinists. Instead it must be approached in the same manner as depth, futurity, beauty and truth. These realities do not present themselves as objects to be grasped, but are known by us only in the non-objecti-

fying mode of being grasped by them. For that reason scientific arguments for or against freedom miss the whole point.

3. See Lawrence Kohlberg, *The Philosophy of Moral Development* (San Francisco: Harper & Row, 1981).
4. Søren Kierkegaard, *The Sickness Unto Death*, in *Fear and Trembling and the Sickness Unto Death*, trans. by Walter Lowrie (New York: Doubleday Anchor Books, 1954), pp. 157–75.
5. Paul Tillich, *The Courage To Be*, pp. 64–85.
6. Ibid., pp. 32ff.
7. Ibid., pp. 36–39.
8. Ibid., pp. 51–57.
9. Ibid., pp. 40–63.
10. Ibid., pp. 32–36.
11. Ibid.
12. Ibid, p. 181.
13. Ernest Becker, *The Denial of Death* (New York: The Free Press, 1973), pp. 127–58.
14. Sigmund Freud, *A General Introduction to Psychoanalysis*, Second Edition, trans. by Joan Riviere (New York: Pocket Books, 1952), pp. 451–52.
15. Becker, p. 142.
16. Ibid., pp. 127–58.
17. Ibid., p. 155.
18. Becker, p. 174. See also Paul Ricoeur, *The Conflict of Interpretations*, pp. 440–67.
19. Becker, pp. 169–70.
20. Quoted by Peter Homans, *Theology After Freud* (Indianapolis: Bobbs-Merrill Co., 1970), p. 78. Italics added.

Chapter 4—Beauty

1. See Louis Dupré, *The Other Dimension* (Garden City, New York: Doubleday & Co., 1972), pp. 228–42.
2. Alfred North Whitehead, *Adventures of Ideas* (New York: The Free Press, 1967), pp. 252–96; *Process and Reality*, corrected edition, ed. by David Ray Griffin and Donald W. Sherburne

(New York: The Free Press, 1978), pp. 62, 183–85, 255 and *passim; Modes of Thought* (New York: The Free Press, 1968), pp. 57–63

3. See Alfred North Whitehead, *Religion in the Making* (New York: Meridian Books, 1960), p. 115.

4. On the significance of narrative see John Navone, S. J. and Thomas Cooper, *Tellers of the Word* (New York: LeJacq Publishing, 1981).

5. For example, Mark Taylor, *Erring: A Postmodern A/theology* (Chicago: University of Chicago Press, 1984).

6. See Taylor, pp. 19–93.

7. In Whitehead's words: "There is then the evil of triviality—a sketch in place of a full picture." Alfred North Whitehead, "Mathematics and the Good," in Paul A. Schillp, ed., *The Philosophy of Alfred North Whitehead* (Evanston and Chicago: Northwestern University Press, 1941), p. 679.

8. Jacques Derrida, *Of Grammatology*, trans. by G. C. Spivak (Baltimore: Johns Hopkins University Press, 1976), pp. 6–26. See also Taylor, pp. 16, 81, 84–85.

9. Taylor, pp. 52–93.

10. Ibid.

11. Ibid. pp. 118, 134 and *passim*.

12. See Whitehead, *Process and Reality*, pp. 110–26; 168–83; *Modes of Thought*, pp. 148–69; and Alfred North Whitehead, *Symbolism* (New York: Capricorn Books, 1959), pp. 12–59.

13. Alfred North Whitehead, *Adventures of Ideas* (New York: The Free Press, 1967), pp. 265, 241–72.

14. See my book, *The Cosmic Adventure* (Ramsey, New Jersey: Paulist Press, 1984), pp. 98–106, 119–37.

15. See Whitehead, *Religion in the Making;* and Alfred North Whitehead, *Science and the Modern World* (New York: The Free Press, 1967), p. 192.

Chapter 5—Truth

1. Søren Kierkegaard, *The Sickness Unto Death*, pp. 175f.

2. This exercise in cognitional self-awareness, and much of the

material in this chapter concerning our "desire to know," is derived from the great cognitional theorist and philosopher, Bernard Lonergan. See especially his book *Insight: A Study of Human Understanding*, 3rd. ed. (New York: Philosophical Library, 1970).

3. For a fuller development of this point see my book, *Religion and Self-Acceptance* (Lanham, Md.: University Press of America, 1980), pp. 7–24.

4. For example, Sigmund Freud, *Civilization and Its Discontents*, trans. by James Strachey (New York: W. W. Norton & Co., 1962); Albert Camus, *The Myth of Sisyphus and Other Essays*, trans. by J. O'Brien (New York: Vintage Books, 1955).

5. The most explicit formulation of an "absurdist" perspective is given in Camus' *The Myth of Sisyphus and Other Essays*.

6. Schubert Ogden, *The Reality of God* (San Francisco: Harper & Row, 1977), p. 34

Conclusion—Mystery

1. See James J. Bacik, *Apologetics and the Eclipse of Mystery* (Notre Dame: University of Notre Dame Press, 1980), pp. 3–64.

2. Ibid.

3. Huston Smith, *Beyond the Post-Modern Mind* (New York: Crossroad, 1982), pp. 83, 88, 114, 134–35.

4. B. F. Skinner, *Beyond Freedom and Dignity* (New York: Bantam Books, 1972), p. 54.

5. On the distinction between problem and mystery see especially Gabriel Marcel, *Being and Having* (Westminster: Dacre Press, 1949), p. 117.

6. My discussion of limit-questions has been influenced especially by David Tracy, *Blessed Rage for Order* (New York: The Seabury Press, 1975), pp. 91–118. The notion of "limiting-questions" comes originally from the philosopher Stephen Toulmin, *An Examination of the Place of Reason in Ethics* (Cambridge: Cambridge University Press, 1970), pp. 202–21.

7. Karl Rahner, *Theological Investigations*, Vol. IV, trans. by

Kevin Smyth (Baltimore: Helicon Press, 1966), pp. 67–73, and Bacik, *passim.*

8. Rahner (ibid.) speaks of three central mysteries in Christian faith. Here, speaking of religion in a general sense, I think it is consistent with Rahner's thought to speak only of two.

9. Rahner (ibid.) The theme of divine self-emptying is one of the major ideas in almost all of Rahner's writings.

10. This formulation is, of course, a Tillichian one.

Index